ALCATRAZ
AT WAR

ALCATRAZ AT WAR

John A. Martini

Golden Gate National Parks Association
San Francisco, California

Library of Congress Control Number 2002108852
ISBN 1-883869-73-0

To Betsy, who makes me believe all things are possible

Contemporary illustrations: Lawrence Ormsby
Design (cover and interior): Carole Thickstun
Editor: Susan Tasaki
Printed on recycled paper in Hong Kong through Global Interprint, Petaluma, California

Cover
*Background, duplicate of frontis; inset, left: illustration by Lawrence Ormsby; inset, right:
PARC, Interpretive Negative Collection, GOGA 2316*

Frontis
Soldiers of the Alcatraz garrison on the island dock, waiting to board the army boat, 1904.

Opposite
*The island's guard detail lined up below the unfinished "bombproof barracks," a vestige of
Civil War construction. The ungainly wooden building looming above served as a barracks
for more than thirty years.*

Company G of the 13th Infantry posed around one of island's few serviceable cannon, a rifled Rodman gun, about 1903. Ironically, this weapon, which was used for training only, faced away from the Golden Gate.

Contents

The Alcatraz warden's house. Originally built as the residence for the commandant of the army's Disciplinary Barracks, this fourteen-room mansion cost $12,000 when completed in 1921.

Introduction

THE WARDEN'S RESIDENCE was the second-most-imposing structure on Alcatraz Island. Built atop a rock outcropping on the island's summit, it was overshadowed only by the hulking yellow-beige cellhouse across the street. Carefully adjusting his Sam Browne belt, the young Coast Artillery officer walked to the front door and rapped sharply on the frame. Never in his most vivid dreams had he envisioned sitting down with the warden of America's notorious federal penitentiary. Things like this didn't happen back in Redwing, Minnesota. Orders were orders, though, and Captain Harry Freeman of the 216th Coast Artillery Regiment had been "invited" to dine with the warden and to discuss the antiaircraft battery he would soon be commanding on top of the prison.

It was June 1942. Much of the Pacific Fleet still lay at the bottom of Pearl Harbor and the US Army was feverishly bolstering West Coast defenses. Alcatraz's location in the center of the harbor made it a perfect gun platform in the event Japanese bombers dared appear over San Francisco Bay. The prison's rooftop was considered to be an especially strategic artillery location, but Warden James A. Johnston had already developed a reputation as a curmudgeon when it came to following the military's wartime regulations. Johnston had recently agreed to the installation of several gun positions on the island, but assuming command of the new battery could turn out to be a ticklish job. Twenty-six-year-old Captain Freeman feared he was in for a long evening.

Alcatraz was going to war. Again.

CAPTAIN HARRY FREEMAN

1

Three GIs of the 216th Coast Artillery regiment and a mechanical gun director atop the guards' apartment house. The director was an early computer that calculated range, direction, and altitude of aircraft and transmitted the data to nearby antiaircraft guns.

THERE IS PROBABLY no more infamous piece of American real estate than Alcatraz Island. Known for decades as "America's Devil's Island" and the "Bastille by the Bay," it served as a prison for nearly all of its recorded history, first as a military stockade for soldier-prisoners then as a federal penitentiary for incorrigible civilian convicts. Although it was only a federal penitentiary for twenty-nine years, that era has become so mythologized in our popular culture that it nearly eclipses all other aspects of Alcatraz history. Almost forgotten today are the island's origin as an impregnable Union fortification during the Civil War and the roles it played as both a fortress and prison during subsequent American wars.

This has not always been a glorious or proud history. During the Civil War and the Indian Wars that followed, the island served both as the largest fortification in the West and as a prison for Union deserters, Confederate spies, Native American warriors, and the criminal dregs of the nation's frontier army. Later, as the country flexed its muscles during the Spanish–American and Philippine wars, hundreds of military prisoners from America's new overseas possessions were shipped to "the Rock."

During World War I, civilians claiming conscientious objector status joined the soldier-prisoners already incarcerated on the island. Called *slackers*—draft dodgers too cowardly to perform their patriotic duty—their beliefs were considered traitorous during a war trumpeted to make the world safe for democracy. They received some of the harshest punishment the US Army could mete out.

The 1940s brought a dual personality to the island, one composed of equal parts patriotism and paranoia. During World War II, young GIs manned antiaircraft guns on top of the prison and waited for an enemy that never came, tossing an occasional surreptitious cigarette to the convicts below. Simultaneously, in the cellblocks and workshops nearby, the "irredeemable types" threw themselves into a furor of war-related work and invested their minuscule salaries in Liberty bonds. Felons though they were, the Alcatraz inmates still considered themselves to be American patriots.

Alcatraz at war was not an attractive place. Wars and prisons seldom are. But throughout its history the island reflected through a gritty mirror something larger than itself: the worst behaviors and, sometimes, the most altruistic goals of America at war.

Convicts weaving rope into cargo nets for the US Navy.

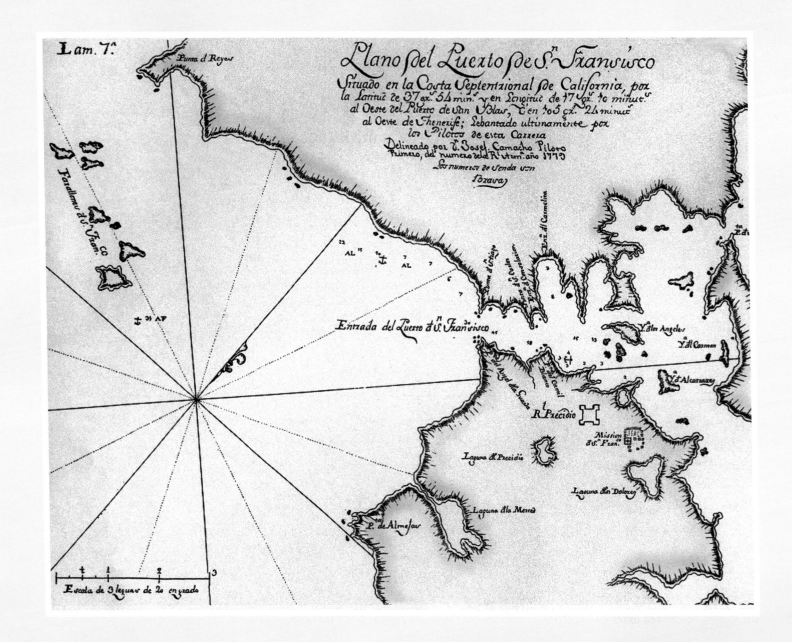

4

Discovery of the Rock

This island is chiefly composed of irregularly stratified sandstone covered with a thin coating of bird guano. The stone is full of seams in all directions which render it unfit for any building purposes.

Lt. William Warner, US Topographical Engineers, 1847[1]

SAN FRANCISCO BAY escaped European notice until 1769, when a Spanish exploring party literally stumbled across its entrance. The explorers, led by Captain Don Gaspar de Portolá, were actually in search of Monterey Bay and had been slogging their way up the California coast for months. Although Spain had claimed this land since 1542, they had not visited Alta (or Upper) California for nearly 150 years. It was terra incognita as far as the foot soldiers were concerned.

In recent years, Russian hunters and traders had begun to appear in Alaska and were slowly expanding their influence down the Pacific coast. Spain feared that without a toehold settlement in California it would lose its nominal claim to the land. Captain Portolá's orders were to locate Monterey Bay and survey the area surrounding it for a future military base. Departing San Diego in early 1769, he had been following the coastline for more than four hundred miles and was becoming increasingly puzzled by his inability to find the bay. In reality, the expedition had already marched right past Monterey Bay without recognizing it. The qualities that had made Monterey so impressive to early Spanish mariners were completely lost on the group of foot soldiers. Portolá's party continued marching north in search of the elusive bay.

One morning in early November, an advance party climbed a coastal ridge and saw a great arm of the sea extending into the land. However, this new bay bore no resemblance

A 1779 map of San Francisco harbor. The Spanish "Alcatrazes" island is at the extreme right, while the future Alcatraz is one of a cluster of four un-named rocks south of Angel Island. (Compare this chart with the army map on page 9.)

to even the wildest descriptions of Monterey, so Portolá figured his real goal must lay still farther north. Attempts to march around the marshy southern end of the estuary quickly demonstrated how big this bay really was. The party's chaplain accurately described it as being so expansive "that not only all the navy of our most Catholic Majesty but those of all Europe could take shelter in it."[2] No matter how vast it might be, though, it still wasn't Monterey Bay. Portolá ordered the expedition to return to Mexico, convinced that he had failed in his primary mission.

Within a few years, other Spanish exploring parties made their ways northward to chart the new bay. On one of these visits, a tiny packet boat named *San Carlos* gingerly felt its way in through the narrows of the harbor mouth and on August 5, 1775, became the first European ship to enter the bay. The *San Carlos* and its captain, Lieutenant Juan Manuel de Ayala, remained in the harbor for six weeks while the ship's pilot charted the bay and its islands. Ayala also exercised the explorer's prerogative of naming every landmark in sight, neglecting to record what the local Ohlone and Miwok tribes might have called them previously. On August 12, he approached a small island "quite barren and rugged and with no shelter for a ship's boats. I named it *Isla de los Alcatraces* [Pelican Island] because of the large number of pelicans that were there."[3] The island Ayala named, though, was actually the island known today as Yerba Buena. Years later, a British mapmaker transposed the name *Alcatraces* to a smaller anonymous island farther to the west. This time the name stuck, and in time became anglicized as "Alcatraz," although for many years the hump-backed rock was also known by such earthy descriptive terms as Bird Island, Guano Island, and White Island.[4]

When the United States conquered California in 1846 during the Mexican War, one of the first orders of government business was to survey the harbor for potential fortification sites. This was an academic exercise, of course, since fewer than five hundred people lived in the flea-bitten town of San Francisco. The bay—and for that matter, the entire territory

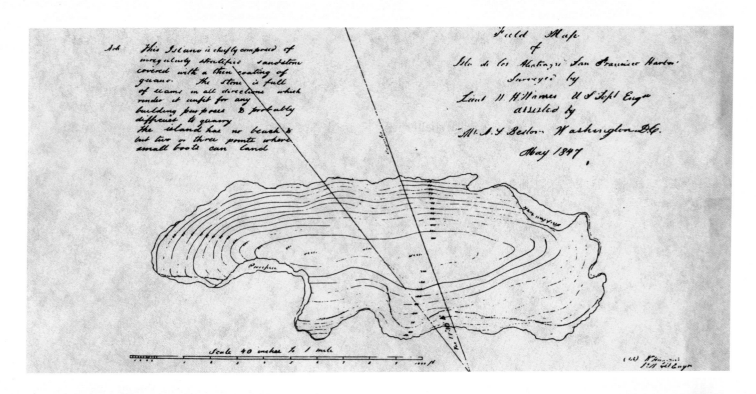

of California—offered little that would put the new American possession at risk from foreign attack.

Everything changed in January 1848 when gold was discovered in the Sierra foothills. Within two years, San Francisco's population exploded by 7,000 percent and hundreds of ships from around the world swung at anchor in its harbor. Seemingly overnight, San Francisco had become the most valuable port in the world. Congress quickly gave the bay top priority for construction of new fortifications.

Beginning in 1850, US Army engineers started to develop plans for harbor defense forts around the bay. The most strategic point, they felt, was the narrow entrance channel that had only recently become known as "the Golden Gate." (Old-timers still referred to it as

In 1847, Lt. William Warner carried out the first careful survey of Alcatraz and recorded the island's original shape. In its natural state, Alcatraz had a jagged shoreline; untold quantities of rock, cut by military convicts from the higher slopes, were used to fill and smooth its perimeter.

Mortar Battery

Battery Rosecranz

Battery Tower

Battery McClellan

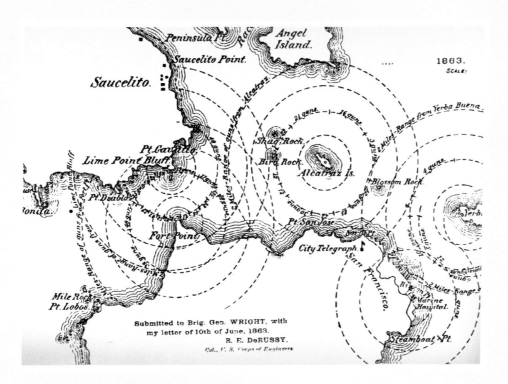

Left
General George Wright's 1863 plan for defending the harbor focused on the Golden Gate. However, the batteries at Lime Point in Marin and on Yerba Buena Island and Rincon Point in San Francisco were never constructed. Instead, the army built temporary batteries in 1864 on Angel Island and Point San Jose in San Francisco to intersect with gunfire from Alcatraz.

Opposite
In 1864, an enterprising photographic company in San Francisco received permission to photograph Alcatraz's defenses. When the Secretary of War heard about the photos, he ordered the series suppressed and all prints destroyed. Some views escaped destruction, and have since surfaced in odd places; these four views were found in the National Archives, mislabeled "Fort Winfield Scott."

Clockwise from upper left
A pair of 10-inch mortars mounted near the lighthouse on the island's summit; Battery Rosecranz at the north end of the island facing Angel Island and the Marin shore; Battery McClellan and a wooden soldiers' barracks at the southern tip of the island; and a row of 32-pounder guns in Battery Tower on the western edge of the island, with the south caponiere in the far distance.

simply *la boca*—"the mouth.") Here the planners recommended two multistory masonry forts, one on each shore of the narrowest part of the straits. These forts, only a mile apart, would hold nearly three hundred cannon and could provide a devastating crossfire at the harbor entrance. If an attacking ship somehow made it through this firestorm, an inner line of fortifications—a third fort on Alcatraz Island and smaller batteries in San Francisco and Marin—would deal with the threat.[5]

In 1853, work began at Alcatraz Island on construction of a series of gun batteries that would encircle the island. Throughout the 1850s, labor crews of busted gold miners excavated roads and gun emplacements around the island's

perimeter and tunneled into its sandstone cliffs to carve out water cisterns and storage rooms. Not satisfied that the rocky heights gave sufficient protection to the gun batteries, army engineers also constructed tall sandstone-and-brick "scarp walls" along much of the island's shoreline.

By the time work was completed in 1859, nearly a half-mile of masonry walls girdled Alcatraz, with gun emplacements behind them for more than one hundred artillery pieces. At several points, defensive towers jutted out from the main walls; these held smaller cannon that provided flanking fire along their exterior faces. A guardhouse with a moat and drawbridge straddled the road leading to the batteries and the top of the island, where a whitewashed lighthouse and a "citadel," or defensive barracks, occupied the summit. In this first incarnation, Alcatraz looked more like a fortified medieval town than a US Army post.

Alcatraz received its first garrison of soldiers on December 30, 1859, when eighty-six men of Company I, 3rd US Artillery moved into its barracks. Transferred from the Washington Territory, the artillerymen had the distinction of occupying the only permanent American fort on the West Coast. Before the day was done, though, eleven soldiers would experience a less pleasant notoriety when they found themselves confined in the island's new guardhouse, the first prisoners ever confined on Alcatraz.

Alcatraz's profile in 1863 was dominated by the lighthouse and three-story citadel atop the summit. Masonry defensive walls lined the vulnerable eastern face of the island with the north caponiere at the right and the guardhouse and its wooden cellblock at center. Other wood-frame buildings on the dock and lining the roads served as workshops, storehouses, and enlisted men's living quarters.

The Civil War

The order of the President suspending the writ of habeas corpus and directing the arrest of all persons guilty of disloyal practices will be rigidly enforced. Those of them who are leading secessionists will be confined at Alcatraz.

Headquarters, Department of the Pacific, 12 September 1862[6]

PERHAPS NOTHING BETTER ILLUSTRATES San Francisco's remoteness from the rest of the United States than the start of the Civil War. On April 12, 1861, Confederate forces in South Carolina fired on Fort Sumter in the middle of Charleston harbor. The rest of the country learned of the outbreak of war within hours. It took twelve days for the news to reach California via Pony Express rider.

San Franciscans never felt more isolated. The US Army began preparations for eventual attack, either by Confederate forces or an uprising of local southern sympathizers. There was also the very real possibility that Great Britain might ally herself with the new Confederate States of America. If that occurred, the Royal Navy's powerful Pacific fleet might well try to capture San Francisco and turn it over to the Confederacy.

San Francisco's defenses were weak, and the bay held many juicy targets for Confederate or British attackers. Aside from the gold and silver mines of the Sierra, the bay area's wealth included innumerable banks, shipyards, warehouses, and factories that had sprouted during the 1850s. The United States government had also erected important installations on the bay: an arsenal, a

The view from the island's South Battery looking back toward the San Francisco waterfront and Telegraph Hill.

Opposite
Alcatraz Island from North Point on the San Francisco waterfront in the 1860s. Dimly visible behind Alcatraz are Belvedere Island (left) and part of Angel Island (right).

navy yard, numerous lighthouses, and even a branch of the US Mint. The worst possible scenario would be that they came under Confederate control.

In the capital at Sacramento, Union politicians warned of the possibility of hostile actions on the part of Secessionists living within the state. Their fears weren't unfounded. San Francisco's population at the time numbered nearly 50,000 people, many of whom were Southern-born. Elsewhere in the state, small but vocal groups of pro-Confederate Copperheads were actively trying to rouse anti-Union sentiments. Their goal was to bring California into the Confederacy and use its reserves of wealth and industry to finance the "War for States' Rights."

The army's original plan for protecting the bay with three large forts and smaller back-up batteries had never been fully implemented; only Alcatraz Island in the middle of the bay stood complete and armed. The situation at the Golden Gate was very different. There at the straits, where a withering crossfire between two forts was the key to defense, only the Presidio's Fort Point had been completed. Work on the companion fort on the northern Marin shore had not even been started due to ongoing disputes over title to the land. Without this second fort, the army feared that on an incoming tide, a swift ship might be able to get past Fort Point and through the Golden Gate.

As a result, the army decided to expand the fortifications on Alcatraz Island to deal with an enemy fleet inside the harbor. Even before the outbreak of war, work had begun on additional island batteries facing due west toward the Gate. When war broke out, 77 cannon were already emplaced on the island—a number that would swell to 104 by the time the war ended four years later. The army began planning to construct four additional back-up batteries in San Francisco and on Angel Island; these would provide intersecting fire with Alcatraz's batteries.

The soldiers on Alcatraz realized their precarious position. On April 27, 1861, artilleryman Charles Herzog wrote his family in Germany: "Well, they even conquered Fort Sumter. The North is against the South. I just hope that we will not have to face these

Two soldiers from the 3rd US Artillery pose alongside the Columbiad cannon of Battery Prime. The rammer staffs, maneuvering spikes, stacks of ammunition, and tin "vent covers" strapped to the cannon's breeches indicate that the guns are ready for instant use. The circular gun platforms allowed the weapons to be rotated 360 degrees.

evils here in California. Everything is in preparation to defend against an attack, but at this time we are sort of safe on our island. The civil war is very unfortunate for America. We do have a hard time with working and shooting, but our batteries could repel a whole fleet."[7]

Colonel Albert Sydney Johnston, the commanding officer of the army's Department of the Pacific, also saw the island as a sort of impregnable warehouse surrounded by the bay. Fearful of Secessionist raids against the Benicia Arsenal, he transferred 10,000 rifles and 150,000 rounds of ammunition to Alcatraz for safekeeping. (Ironically, Johnston was a Southerner who later resigned from the US Army to fight and die for the Confederacy. Until relieved of his California command in late April 1861, though, Johnston did everything he could to protect Union forts from rebel attack.)

As the number of guns and batteries on Alcatraz continued to swell, so did the number of prisoners locked up on the island. Every army post of the era had a prison room in its guardhouse for confining unruly soldiers, and Alcatraz's was the strongest in the West. Located on an island in a bay, the guardhouse was deemed almost escape-proof. Shortly after the island was garrisoned in 1859, other army posts began sending their most hardcore soldier-prisoners to Alcatraz. The first such convict arrived only two months after the island opened—Private Matthew Hayland, "an insane man delivered for confinement and safekeeping awaiting transfer to Washington." This practice of holding non-garrison prisoners became formalized on August 27, 1861, when the island was designated the official military prison for the Department of the Pacific.[8]

Not long after the outbreak of war, the military also began locking up particularly outspoken civilians whose views were deemed dangerous or traitorous. At one point this included Mr. C. L. Weller, the chairman of the State Democratic Committee and former governor of California, who was arrested after making

The citadel originally served as combination officers' quarters, enlisted men's barracks, post headquarters, and hospital. By the time this picture was taken in the 1880s, its interior had been converted to six three-story "townhouse" apartments for junior officers, each with its own wooden entry portico spanning the moat.

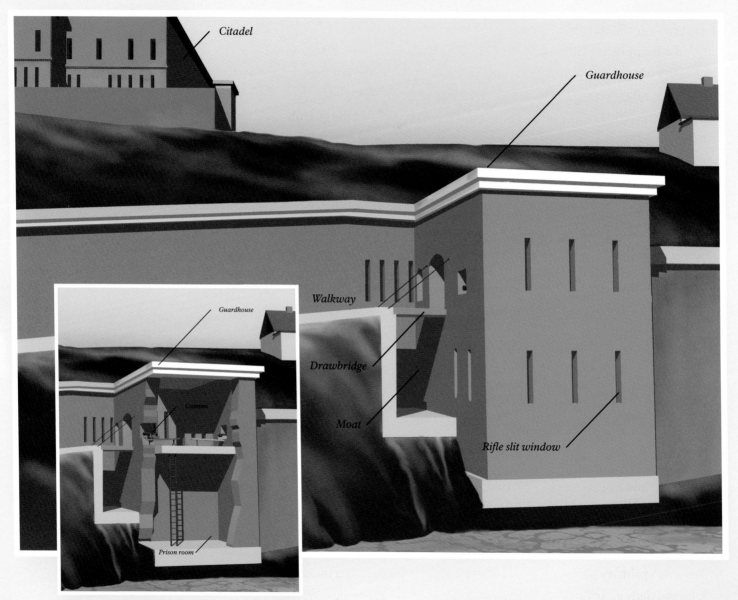

Citadel

Guardhouse

Walkway

Drawbridge

Moat

Rifle slit window

Guardhouse

Caisson

Prison room

an especially incendiary speech during the 1864 presidential campaign. (Weller was released after posting a $25,000 bond and swearing an oath of allegiance to the Union.)

These early prisoners found themselves confined in a bare room in the basement of the guardhouse, allowed outside only for intermittent exercise. The prison room, measuring 20 feet by 11 feet, was entered through a trapdoor in the floor of the guardhouse and an iron ladder down into the depths. Within its confines, up to forty men at a time slept on blankets or straw pallets on the floor. There was no sanitation or running water in the prison room, and the only light and air came through barred rifle slits in the walls. Living conditions in this hole can only be grimly imagined. By the fall of 1861, severe outbreaks of illness among both the civilian and military prisoners were reported, and the departmental commander ordered the convicts moved into tents so that a thorough "cleansing of the prison room" could be carried out.

In March 1863, a group of Secessionists almost succeeded in bringing the Civil War to California. These men had organized themselves into a secret society called the Knights of the Golden Circle and had clandestinely outfitted the schooner *J. M. Chapman* with a cache of arms, cannon, and ammunition. Their goal was to sail outside the Golden Gate, capture an ocean-going steamship, and take it to Mexico, where it would be outfitted as a Confederate warship. The converted man-of-war would then raid Yankee commerce in the Pacific and attempt to blockade San Francisco Bay.

The military got wind of the conspiracy, though, and on the night she was scheduled to sail, the *Chapman* was captured by a navy warship. The crew of fifteen was arrested and the schooner and its cargo towed to Alcatraz. The ringleaders ended up in the island guardhouse, where they were held during questioning. Eventually tried and convicted of treason (the jury needing only four minutes to return a guilty verdict), the conspiracy's leaders were saved from ten-year sentences on the island by a pardon from President Lincoln.[9]

Alcatraz's primary mission was still harbor defense, though, and the cannon shots boomed out daily as artillerymen practiced by firing at targets on nearby Angel Island.

The island's guardhouse was a self-contained fortification in its own right, complete with dry moat, drawbridge, and positions for riflemen on its open roof. Three howitzers on the first floor protected the roads and defensive walls on either side of the guardhouse, while the bare basement room served as a prison room for the island's garrison.

It was often a hazardous profession. Private Herzog wrote home about one memorable artillery practice in 1861:

> Everybody was at their places. The officer gave the command "Number one, fire!" But as soon as the command was given our cannon did explode and the pieces were flying around in the air. My clothes were ripped off my body, my pants and jacket were hanging in rags. For several days I was half-deaf. . . . Everybody thought I was dead and when I climbed out of the rubble there was loud cheering. Everyone said I could face any fire now because no bullet would be able to injure me; it was really a miracle that none of the others around had been injured.[10]

One of duties assigned to Alcatraz's garrison was to ensure that ships arriving in the bay complied with all military orders regarding inspections and berthing assignments. One Indian summer day in October 1863, an unidentified warship was spotted under tow near Sausalito, headed for the channel leading to the Mare Island Shipyard. "I could distinguish a flag flying at her peak," wrote the island's commander, Captain William Winder, "but there being no wind, the flag fell in folds rendering it impossible to determine her nationality. The direction taken by the ship being so unusual I deemed it my duty to bring her to and ascertain her character."[11]

Winder's solution was to fire a blank cannon to get the ship's attention, followed shortly by a shot across her bow when the warship failed to respond. The vessel turned out to be HMS *Sutlej*, the flagship of the British navy's Pacific Squadron, commanded by a very irate Admiral John Kingcome, who wanted to know why he had been fired upon by a supposedly friendly fort. Official correspondence flew between the British ship and the US Army, with the upshot being that the Admiral was formally reminded of wartime harbor regulations. Captain Winder received a veiled reprimand for his actions and was advised that in the future, "It is expected that the delicate duty devolving on military commanders will be exercised with prudence."[12]

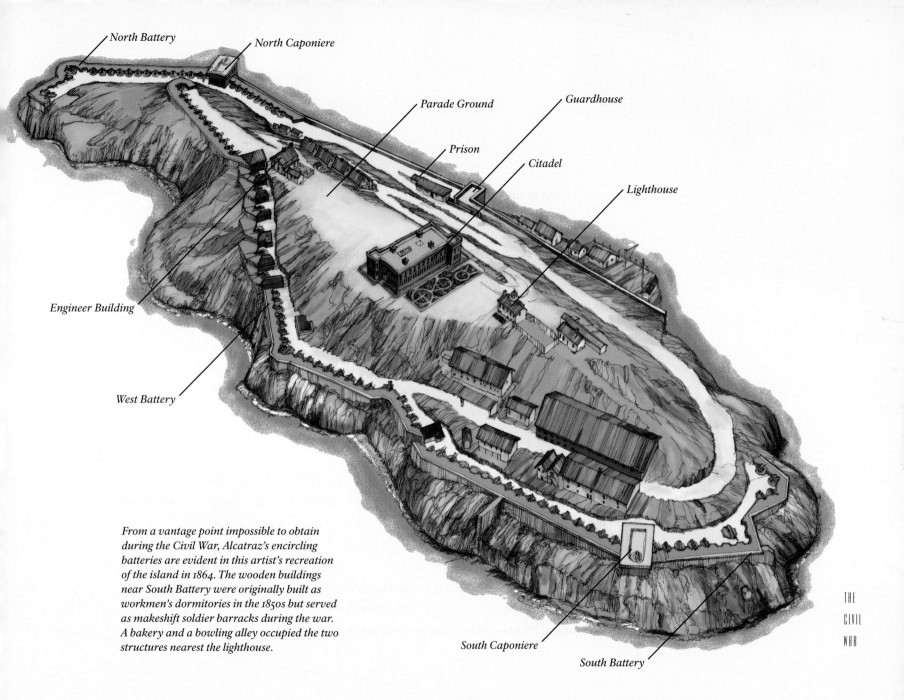

North Battery

North Caponiere

Parade Ground

Guardhouse

Prison

Citadel

Lighthouse

Engineer Building

West Battery

From a vantage point impossible to obtain
during the Civil War, Alcatraz's encircling
batteries are evident in this artist's recreation
of the island in 1864. The wooden buildings
near South Battery were originally built as
workmen's dormitories in the 1850s but served
as makeshift soldier barracks during the war.
A bakery and a bowling alley occupied the two
structures nearest the lighthouse.

South Caponiere

South Battery

Island families lovingly planted a tiny garden between the lighthouse and the citadel in the 1860s. With an eye towards practicality, the gardens sat directly atop the island's water cisterns on a flat area originally intended as an ordnance storage yard. Soil for the garden was apparently imported from nearby Angel Island, where the Alcatraz garrison maintained a large vegetable patch.

Alcatraz's impressive 15-inch Rodman cannon were a favorite subject of San Francisco photographer Eadweard Muybridge, who extensively documented the island following the Civil War. The army, easing its restrictive wartime policies, allowed Muybridge to sell stereographic views of the island to the public starting in 1869.

The number of men assigned to Alcatraz swelled throughout the Civil War, reaching a high point of 433 men in early 1865. New recruits were continually arriving on the island and undergoing training before being shipped out to patrol the Southwest frontier. (Few Californians actually saw combat on eastern battlefields.) The fortifications also continued to grow both in the number of cannons and their sizes, culminating in 15-inch caliber Rodman guns capable of flinging a 440-pound cannonball more than three miles. By mid-1865, five of these monsters had been hauled onto the island.

The Civil War ended on April 9, 1865. Six days later, Abraham Lincoln was assassinated. This time the news reached California almost immediately over the transcontinental telegraph, and the fort's soldiers were ferried to San Francisco to enforce law and order. Crowds of Unionists sacked pro-Confederate newspapers that night, and throughout California there were men "so utterly infamous as to exult over the assassination of the President." Soldiers took these men into custody before the mobs could reach them, and thirty-nine ended up on Alcatraz, where the army immediately put them to work constructing new defenses.

Alcatraz was given the duty of firing a half-hourly mourning gun for the slain president, and its troops marched in a mass memorial procession through the city on April 19. Several weeks later, a journalist visited the island and chronicled the fate of the Secessionists still confined there. He reported the men were working under armed guard excavating foundations for a new battery near the island's wharf. Some were shackled to 24-pound iron balls to restrict their movement, and anyone refusing to work was locked in a strap-iron "sweat box" barely tall enough to allow a prisoner inside to stand erect. The reporter also took pains to describe how the Secessionists drank coffee made out of used grounds. Although Alcatraz stood at its high point as a harbor fortification, it was this gang of convicts sweating down by the dock that foreshadowed the island's most important role in years to come.

A pro-Union rally on Market Street in San Francisco during the Civil War.

One of the island's last army officers posed for a 1933 news photo on an aging Rodman cannon, embedded in the parade ground wall as an ornament.

The Guns of Alcatraz

Although Alcatraz was never totally armed (few American forts were), the island still bristled with an impressive array of 19th-century ordnance on the eve of the Civil War. Cannon during this period were generally classified according to the diameter of their bores or the weight of the projectiles they fired, and Alcatraz's guns ranged in size from relatively small 24-pounder howitzers up through 10-inch Columbiad pattern cannon.

Each of the island's guns was designed to fire a variety of destructive projectiles. The simplest type of cannonball was a solid, round iron ball called a shot, but most of the fort's guns were designed to also fire hollow explosive balls called shells. Fitted with slow-burning fuses, shells were timed to detonate just as they hit the target and were preferred by gunners for shattering ships' rigging or clearing decks of sailors.

Perhaps the oddest type of projectile available to Alcatraz's gunners was "hot shot." Behind the island's main batteries stood two furnaces in which solid cannonballs could be heated until cherry red. The hot shot were then quickly loaded into a nearby cannon and fired. When the red-hot iron cannonball hit a wooden ship, it would bury itself in the hull and set the vessel afire. Heated shot could even be skipped across wave tops to hit an attacker close to the waterline.

Alcatraz's smallest guns were the 24-pounder howitzers mounted in the island's guardhouse and in the masonry towers known as caponieres that jutted from the North and South batteries. Although capable of firing cannonballs, the howitzers were positioned for close-in defense against landing parties and were usually loaded with either grapeshot or canister. These murderous loads consisted of clusters of small balls that sprayed out of a cannon's muzzle with a devastating, shotgun-like effect. Canister shot was

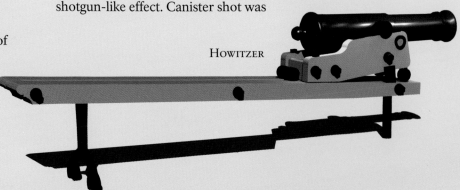

HOWITZER

especially feared; when fired at close range it was capable of tearing infantrymen to pieces.

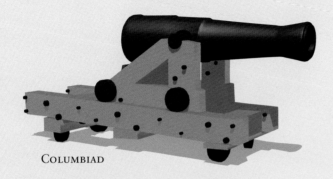

COLUMBIAD

The mainstays of Alcatraz's weaponry were the large smoothbore guns designed in the 1840s known as Columbiads. Mounted in the open barbette batteries that encircled the island, most of the Columbiads were 8-inch caliber models capable of firing a 64-pound cannonball. At key points in the island's defenses, such as at the angles of the batteries, 10-inch caliber Columbiads firing 128-pound shot were emplaced. With a well-trained gun crew, a Columbiad could hit a target at a range of two miles about 10 percent of the time. (At closer range, of course, results were much better.) This inherent inaccuracy led to the clustering of dozens of Columbiads in the island's batteries to multiply their firepower.

Midway through the Civil War, new guns of an 1861 pattern known as Rodmans were installed in many of the island's batteries. More sleek than the earlier pattern cannon mounted before the Civil War, these guns reflected the improved design and casting techniques of American foundries. Many of the Rodmans were 8- and 10-inch caliber and were emplaced alongside the earlier Columbiads.

However, due to the island's critical defensive role, in 1864 the army sent Alcatraz a pair of the largest weapons then in production: 15-inch Rodman weighing 50,000 pounds that could fire a solid shot three miles. At that range, no vessel in any navy could withstand the meteoric impact of the 440-pound projectile.

As the war progressed, the island's strategic importance became increasingly apparent and more and more weapons were sent to the island: horse-drawn field pieces, additional Rodman cannon, navy guns originally intended for shipboard use, mortars, and various styles of early rifled cannon. By 1866 the Alcatraz batteries held 111 cannon—the greatest number of weapons ever mounted on the island.

RODMAN

27

The post headquarters building (left) and "Officers' Row" (right), about 1885. The army constructed three Victorian-style residences in 1880 for the island's senior staff, who had previously lived in cramped quarters in the citadel.

The Indian Wars

Along the roadside, as it nears the summit, are a succession of charming gothic cottages occupied by the commanding officers of the garrison and their families, each with a little garden plot, and the voices of merry children make the air musical.

Daily Alta California, *August 2, 1885*

FOLLOWING THE CIVIL WAR, the United States entered a period of thirty years when it was not involved in any foreign wars. It would be the longest period of peace in the young nation's history. However, the country was not free from internal military actions, for this was the era known as the Indian Wars, a time of continual skirmishes between frontier troops and Native American warriors. Throughout these decades, the army established scores of small Western forts from which troops tried vainly to maintain order on the frontier and prevent clashes between the native people and settlers who were encroaching on their lands. The soldiers also had the unenviable task of making sure the tribes remained on the often-worthless reservations established for them by Congress.

When Native Americans attempted to flee these reservations, the soldiers forced them back. It was a frustrating "war" for the US Army. There was no identifiable army for them to confront, nor were there any defined front lines where soldiers fought hand-to-hand over a piece of real estate. Instead, it was a

The entrance to Lower Prison appeared as a menacing portal in the island's brickwork. Construction on the haphazard prison complex began during the Civil War and continued through the turn of the century; it eventually comprised more than a dozen firetrap cellblocks and support buildings.

This highly romanticized 1870s engraving only hints at the large number of buildings that actually dotted Alcatraz. By contrast, the artist was fastidiously accurate in his depiction of the fishing boats and sailing ships in the bay.

Then as now, a switchback roadway led to the top of the island. In this 1880s view, "new" officers' quarters line the roadway at center while the citadel sits on the hill at the right. The roofs of the enlisted men's barracks and prison buildings are visible at lower left.

desert and wilderness war of endless patrols, dirt, tedium, hit-and-run firefights, and terrifying brutality on both sides.

Hampered by budget cuts and hard-pressed to keep its posts garrisoned, the army frequently lowered its standards to meet manpower goals. There was no draft during this era, and recruiting officers would overlook physical and mental defects to fill regimental ranks. Many new recruits were immigrants who spoke little or no English, while others had criminal histories and enlisted under assumed identities in the hope of dodging the law.

On Alcatraz Island, these lowered standards soon became evident as soldier-prisoners began to arrive from all over the West. Generally the most refractory thieves, deserters, drunks, and violent soldiers in the army, many were also classified as "feeble minded," or insane, by the post surgeon. By 1870 the prison population had swollen to 153 inmates.[13]

The prisoners had long ago overflowed the old prison room and were now housed in a complex of wooden cellblocks adjacent to the original guardhouse. During the 1870s and 1880s, additional buildings were haphazardly constructed in this area until much of the island's lee shore was covered by barn-like prison structures. "Lower Prison," as it came to be known, eventually included four cavernous cell blocks, each containing dozens of wooden cells with iron grill doors. In 1881 the post surgeon recorded the average cell dimensions as 6 feet deep by 3 feet wide, with 8-foot-high ceilings.[14]

An armed sentry walks his post atop the roof of Lower Prison in 1893. The brick structure at the center of the complex was constructed in 1867 as Alcatraz's first permanent cellblock, but hurriedly built wooden additions soon engulfed it. By the time this photo was taken, the old cellblock had been converted into a day room for the guard staff.

Alcatraz's days as a harbor fortification were already beginning to wane. The fort had reached its zenith in 1866 when 111 heavy guns were mounted in its batteries, but most of these were deemed totally ineffective against modern ironclad warships. Even the batteries themselves were considered obsolete, their towering masonry walls seen as little more than inviting targets for long-range guns. The army came to the rueful conclusion that the entire fort would have to be demolished and rebuilt. It had a ready source of manpower for this daunting task—the convicts locked in the hodgepodge of prison structures down by the guardhouse. Shortly after the Civil War ended, they were put to work tearing down old masonry walls and magazines and modernizing the batteries. In order to reduce the island's profile, they also began hacking and cutting its rocky slopes and tossing the spoil along the shore. In one memorable effort, convict workers using nothing more than hand

Quarrying and breaking rock served as never-ending punishments for the soldier-prisoners on Alcatraz. Eadweard Muybridge titled this 1869 photograph of a convict work party "Military Exercises at Alcatraz"— a sarcastic comment on the island's penal role. (Muybridge's photos of military exercises at other army posts invariably showed troops lined up in starched-perfect formations.)

tools and pushcarts leveled a 60-foot-high slope to create a parade ground at the south end of the island.

The army soon realized that the convicts were a valuable labor pool for other military projects around the bay. Before long, prisoners were being ferried to the Presidio, Marin County, and Angel Island, where they worked at tasks ranging from quarrying rocks to tending vegetable gardens.

Considered unfit to dress like regular soldiers, the prisoners wore discarded uniforms without any insignia and from which all brass buttons had been removed. Eventually, their status became even more identifiable when the large white letter P was painted or sewn on their jackets and hats.

Although many soldiers arrived on Alcatraz bearing scars of military-issued brandings or tattooing, there are no records that this type of corporal punishment actually took place on the island. Prisoners who refused to work were either confined in their cells or hauled off to closet-sized "dungeon rooms" (the official designation) inside the old 1859 guardhouse.

Native American prisoners, warriors captured during various military campaigns, were also sent to the island. The first of these was "Paiute Tom," who arrived on Alcatraz on June 5, 1873, only to be killed by a guard two days later while attempting escape. In October that same year, two Modocs— Barncho and Sloluck—who had participated in an attack on peace commissioners during the Modoc War arrived on the Rock to serve life sentences. They had originally been

By 1902, quarrying operations had shifted to the other side of Alcatraz, where these prisoners are cutting rock on the site of the present Industries Building. Rock from Alcatraz was used as paving material at other military posts around the bay.

The Hopi leader Lomahongyoma and his "hostile" conspirators, posed in front of the original Alcatraz lighthouse. When they arrived on the island in January 1895, the island's commanding officer was shocked at their clothing (or rather, lack of it) and ordered them outfitted in recycled army uniforms.

In this view of the "Moqui Indians," Lomahongyoma is wearing his ceremonial chief's robe and carrying an army officer's hat, both probably signs of rank. The army's intent, it seems, was to give the Hopi leader a modicum of dignity.

sentenced to death for the murder of General E. J. Canby, but President Ulysses S. Grant commuted their sentences to life imprisonment on Alcatraz. The army, apparently outraged at the commutation, withheld the news from the men until they were literally at the gallows' steps. (Four other Modocs were hanged simultaneously at Fort Klamath for their roles.) Barncho died of scrofula in 1875 and was buried in the cemetery on Angel Island, while Sloluck eventually had his sentence reduced and rejoined his tribe in 1878. Sloluck's five-year stay was the longest of any Native American in the military prison.[15]

Over the next dozen years at least fifteen more Indians arrived on the island, some of whom were actually Indian scouts employed by the US Army. These men had participated in mutinies against military authority, and their confinement was more in keeping with Alcatraz's role of housing soldier-prisoners rather than POWs.

The water-side of Lower Prison, 1902. The two wooden cellblocks at left are identifiable by their square ventilator openings, while the prison's mess hall and kitchen are situated along the bay edge. The semicircular building at center housed a staircase leading into the mess hall.

The largest number of Indian prisoners arrived in January 1895, when nineteen Moquis (Hopi) from Arizona were sent to the Rock. These men and their leader, Lomahongyoma, had been classified as "hostiles" by the army for their continued resistance to sending their children to a Moqui Indian Agency school and for refusing to cooperate with a government-mandated farming system. They were ordered held on Alcatraz until "they shall show . . . they fully realize the error of their evil ways," and "make proper promise of good behavior in the future."[16] In mid-February, a reporter visited the Hopi and reported that they were engaged in the same type of labor as the soldier-prisoners, including breaking rocks and sawing firewood. "Their work is varied occasionally by little trips to San Francisco, where they are taken to visit the public schools under strict guard, so they can see the harmlessness of the multiplication table in its daily application." Tellingly, the reporter elaborated on the Indians' motives for their continued passive resistance: "Their aversion to the schools where the Government proposed to send their children, was based on the fact that they had seen a number of their offspring die in them from the effects of some contagious disease, and so they laid the deaths at the door of too much learning."[17]

Promises to obey all government orders were eventually extracted from all nineteen of the Hopi, and they remained on Alcatraz until August 3, when word arrived from Washington that they could return to their reservation. It is not known if they "realized the error of their evil ways," but it's safe to assume that after being taken from their homes in Arizona, they long remembered their seven months' confinement on the barren Rock.

The slab-sided wooden cellblocks of Lower Prison gave little hint of the warren of cells inside. In this view, the two largest cellblocks span the roadway while the prison mess hall and washhouse sit at the base of the old defensive wall. In the distance, the original guardhouse is visible, with another cellblock on its roof. The prison's latrine sits on pilings just offshore.

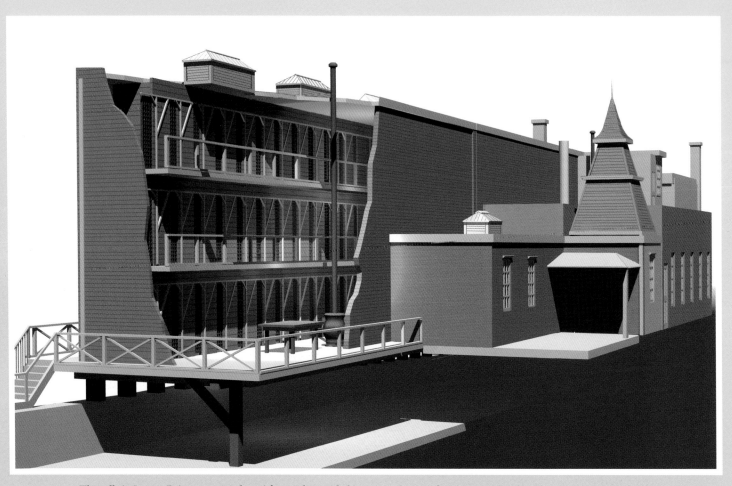

The cells in Lower Prison averaged 3 x 6 feet and provided just enough space for a narrow bunk and a chamber pot. Luckily for the prisoners, they were only locked in their cells at night. During the day, prisoners not assigned to work details were allowed to mingle in the open areas in front of the cells.

Military Justice

Punishments dealt out by the frontier army could be brutal. Although Congress had officially outlawed flogging and branding, officers and non-coms at many forts often overlooked this technicality. Corporal punishment and humiliation seemed obvious treatments for foul-ball soldiers at remote areas that had no guardhouse for locking up prisoners.

Convicted soldiers were often branded or tattooed with the letter D for deserter or T for thief. Marking a man like this served two purposes: it was both a reminder to others of the soldier's crime and it prevented him from re-enlisting under a false name, since a military doctor would immediately spot the telltale brand or tattoo.[18]

Punishments recorded in the 1870s and '80s sound medieval by today's penal standards—tying men up by their thumbs, stretching them over the spare wheels of moving wagons, "bucking and gagging" by tying hands and feet behind their backs and forcing a gag down their throats, and staking them out spread-eagled in the sun or snow.

Lower Prison in early 1902. The belfry at center housed a bell rung to announce fires, escapes, and other emergencies. This photograph is one of a series ordered by the post commandant documenting deplorable conditions on the island. He sent the photos back to Washington in a plea for funds to improve prison conditions on what was already grimly known throughout the US Army as "the Rock."

Military convicts building a foundation for the expansion of Upper Prison.

4 The Spanish-American War and the Philippine Insurrection

As a purely defensive proposition there can be no question that the installation of high power guns on Alcatraz Island would not only greatly strengthen but would make the defense of San Francisco Bay absolutely invincible against any combination that the entire world could bring against it. . . . All of Alcatraz should be devoted to fortifications. . . . The island shall be dedicated exclusively and for all time to purposes of defense.

Major General Arthur MacArthur, 1903[19]

THE WINDING-DOWN of the Indian Wars in the early 1890s brought both a decrease in the number of prisoners on Alcatraz and a fading of the island's role as a harbor defense fort. As the Indian campaigns ended, the army closed dozens of lesser frontier posts and centralized its cavalry and infantry regiments at larger forts with more permanent facilities (including guardhouses). On Alcatraz, the crowding in the wooden cellblocks decreased from a record-high population of 177 men in March 1872 to an average of only 35 men during the 1890s.

At the same time that the prison seemed to be shrinking in importance, the army was reevaluating the island's historic role as a fortification. Work had slowed to a standstill on remodeling the pre-Civil War batteries, and only nine Rodman cannon remained on the island. Beginning in 1886 the country had begun a complete modernization of its harbor

Lower Prison, as viewed from the guards' barracks. The small building in the foreground housed the "Alcatraz Press" printing shop. The large brick structure behind it served as a combination chapel/library/theater for the prison.

defenses, and the military's plans for San Francisco dictated that new fortifications should be clustered near the Golden Gate. Although Alcatraz still held a commanding position in the center of the bay, army engineers argued over whether or not guns mounted on the island would have much strategic value.

Any doubts about the future use of Alcatraz came to a dramatic halt in 1898 with the outbreak of the Spanish–American War. The sinking of the battleship *Maine* in Havana Harbor in February 1898 cut deeply into the American psyche. Fueled by a mix of patriotism and jingoistic enthusiasm, American men volunteered by the tens of thousands to liberate Spanish colonial possessions. As William Randolph Hearst put it, "America was spoiling for a fight and Spain would do as well as anyone." Recruits soon began pouring into San Francisco to await transport to Guam and the Philippine Islands.

On Alcatraz, the war's first effect was a rapid rotation of personnel as troops shipped out to the western Pacific. The turnover was so rapid that the island had thirteen commanding officers between 1898 and 1900. Remaining stocks of ammunition and ordnance stores were stripped from the island and sent to Cuba and the Philippines. As it had during the Civil War, the island again became a recruit depot for California Volunteer units awaiting training and transport.[20] Work also began on emplacements for two 8-inch rifled cannon on the west side of the island positioned to protect a new underwater mine field planted in the bay between the island and the Golden Gate.

The war was so short, though, that the mines were barely wet and the volunteers not yet in their temporary camps before Admiral Dewey decimated the Spanish Fleet in a lopsided turkey shoot in

A pair of 15-inch Rodman guns at the south end of the island, about 1900. By the time this photo was taken the cannon were obsolete, replaced by "modern" fortifications located outside the Golden Gate.

Manila Harbor just two days after war was declared. For all intents and purposes, the real fighting in the Pacific was over before the first US soldier set foot on a transport ship. When American soldiers finally did arrive in the Philippines, they found themselves in the awkward role of an army of occupation, not of liberation.

The war against Spain officially ended on December 10, 1898, but not the fighting in the Philippine Islands. Filipino nationalists had been struggling against colonial rule for decades and they were not about to trade foreign domination by a European monarchy for foreign domination by an

Top
Officers of the island's garrison, displaying a fine array of uniform styles and gold braid, pose for an informal portrait.

Bottom
Lighthouse and keepers, with the citadel in the background.

American democracy. Violence against the occupying American troops broke out almost immediately in what quickly became known as the Philippine Insurrection.[21]

On Alcatraz, the war had been so brief that the 8-inch guns were never even mounted in the new battery. However, the after-effects of the war and insurrection would soon sweep over the island as a delayed deluge of military prisoners arrived from the Pacific. By late 1899, the number of convicts had already increased to more than 150 men when word arrived that transports were en route from Manila carrying 135 more prisoners. The Departmental Commanding General immediately wired Washington for more construction funds; the influx of prisoners, he announced, would outstrip the existing prison's capacity by a factor of three.

Almost immediately, work began on constructing another complex of cellblocks to augment the Lower Prison facilities. The new prison, located on the convict-created parade ground at the southern end of the island, eventually included three wooden cellblocks, a washhouse, workshops, and a new guardhouse, all enclosed by a stockade wall and a guards' walkway. The compound, however, did not include any mess facilities, so the convicts had to be marched to Lower Prison three times a day under armed guard for their meals. The new buildings and wooden stockade (whose architecture resembled something more appropriate to a frontier trading post than a California artillery fort) soon became known as "Upper Prison."

By April 1900, the convict population reached a new high of 441 men, many of whom had committed serious crimes against fellow

Prisoners at work in Upper Prison. Three men are breaking rocks by hand while the fourth is knocking mortar off used bricks and piling them for future reuse.

Opposite
More views from the 1902 photographic series documenting Lower Prison. Top: the interior of one of the two cellblocks that spanned the roadway north of the guardhouse; the façade of the original brick cellblock appears at left. Middle: the prison's kitchen, with a sorry-looking pile of potatoes on the counter at center. Bottom: the mess hall; 200 men could be fed in this narrow building.

Upper Prison and its stockade wall. A guards' walkway circled the entire perimeter.

soldiers and were serving terms ranging from five to twenty years "at hard labor." There were soon more prisoners on the island than available work, so increasingly, convict work crews were dispatched to army posts around the bay. The little steamship *General McDowell* shuttled constantly between Alcatraz and the other installations, transporting prisoners who labored at road construction, rock-breaking, brush-clearing, trash-hauling, and other menial tasks before being returned to their cells each night. It is estimated that more than 2,500 soldiers served time in Upper and Lower prisons by the time the Philippine Insurrection ended in 1903.

As these back-to-back conflicts progressed, it became obvious to all concerned that the island's role as a prison now far overshadowed its value as a fortification. Shortly after 1900, the army dropped any pending plans for new batteries on Alcatraz and in July 1907, the post name was officially changed to "Pacific Branch, US Military Prison, Alcatraz Island." In future years, the aging Rodman guns sitting in the shadow of Upper Prison would serve only as martial ornaments for passing military convict work gangs.

Stretcher-bearers from the island's medical detachment.

5 World War I

The Stone Which the Builders Rejected has Become
the Head of the Arch

Inspirational motto painted over the doorway to the Disciplinary Barracks mess hall

"THE GREAT WAR" was a bad time to be a conscientious objector. In 1917, the United States Congress voted to finally join in the war that had been raging in Europe for three years, and citizens around the country responded patriotically once more and volunteered for military service by the thousands. When these numbers weren't enough to fill the military's projected needs, additional men were conscripted into the armed forces through a civilian draft administered by the Selective Service Bureau.

Not all the men who were drafted, however, believed in the principles of "The War to End All Wars." Hundreds of Americans rejected military service altogether and denounced the war on either religious or political grounds. In an era when anti-German sentiment ran so high that sauerkraut was renamed Liberty Cabbage and dachshunds were kicked in the streets, taking an anti-war stance was a perilous career choice. The resistors called themselves conscientious objectors, or COs, but the public referred to them derogatorily as slackers.

The COs took the route of passive resistance. They dutifully reported to their draft boards when called up, but they refused to take any pledges swearing allegiance to the armed forces or follow any military orders. Their refusals were seen as disobedience to military law. Philip Grosser, an avowed anarchist, summarized his position concisely:

The island's appearance changed drastically in the early 20th century when permanent concrete buildings replaced earlier structures. In this 1926 view, the lighthouse and light keepers' quarters are at center with the Disciplinary Barracks directly behind. The new commandant's residence is at right. The 60-foot cut excavated by prisoners fifty years earlier is plainly visible.

49

The view down the island's switchback roadway in the mid-1880s . . .

and the same view in the early 1920s. Lower Prison has totally disappeared, and only the old hospital on the hill remains unchanged. The island's Post Exchange (at center, with the sign reading "Soldiers Club") provided enlisted soldiers with amenities that included a convenience store, cafeteria, barbershop, bowling alleys, and gym. The stucco building behind the trees at right originally served as an armory and cobbler shop.

After I registered for the draft as an objector to war on political grounds, I refused to submit to physical examination for military purposes and refused to sign an enlistment and assignment card. Instead of being tried for violation of the wartime conscription act, which was a Federal civil offense, I was turned over to the military and was subjected to all forms of punishment as an erring soldier. . . [22]

In short, Grosser and other conscientious objectors were punished as soldiers who violated military regulations rather than as civilians who refused to become soldiers. And whether the objectors acknowledged it or not, the army sent soldiers who violated regulations to military prisons.

Between 1917 and 1920, Alcatraz Island would house scores of slackers whose positions ranged from Grosser's militant anarchism to the religious nonviolence of Quakers and Hutterites. Once on the island, most objectors continued to refuse all compliance with military authority; the men would not drill nor respond to orders nor wear an army uniform, even a prison one. They were, in short, a pain in the neck to the island's commanding officer.

Since 1915, Alcatraz had been known as "Pacific Branch, US Disciplinary Barracks," in keeping with the army's growing acceptance of rehabilitation as the goal of military punishment. Most convicts sent to Alcatraz were now considered to be miscreant soldiers undergoing retraining and discipline rather than simple confinement, and were assigned to "disciplinary companies" while on the island. Unlike earlier years when prisoners were given discarded uniforms emblazoned with a P, men were now allowed to wear a variation of a regular army uniform. Known as "disciples," these men participated in a wide variety of educational classes that included training in both military and vocational skills. Although hard labor was still prescribed in many of their sentences, even this

punishment increasingly took the form of useful skills such as carpentry, blacksmithing, masonry, and tailoring. If a soldier's behavior and attitude improved acceptably while in the disciplinary barracks, he would eventually be transferred back to regular service, albeit with a major black mark on his service record.

In 1918, the Disciplinary Barracks hosted a medical staff numbering 23 officers and enlisted men. Medical treatment provided to army's prisoners included dentistry, physical therapy, and psychiatric care. The island's new hospital, located above the prison mess hall, also included a fully equipped operating room and x-ray lab.

The exceptions to this enlightened policy were the so-called "numbered prisoners," men who had disgraced the army and were referred to only by registry number, never by name. These men had already been convicted of serious offenses by courts martial and would be discharged at the end of their sentences. They were on Alcatraz only to be punished, and worked at humble tasks like breaking rock in the island's quarry. While on Alcatraz, the "numbers" were confined in a different part of the cellhouse and wore all-black uniforms to set them apart from the "disciples" of the disciplinary companies.

The army classified the conscientious objectors on Alcatraz as numbers, since they obviously weren't participating in any of the training classes. Although official records concerning these men have not survived, newspaper stories indicate that nearly a hundred objectors were sent to Alcatraz, most of them transferred from Leavenworth after the end of the war. At times, the objectors received some of the roughest treatment still meted out on the island: solitary confinement in the dungeons below the cellhouse.

Versions of the objectors' experiences on Alcatraz vary wildly according to source. The island newspaper, *The Rock*, printed the official US Army point of view in a 1917 article titled "The Slacker Problem."

They come here charged with the serious offense of desertion in time of war. Such an offense . . . is punishable even by death. These men are not immediately tried and given a sentence of ten or more years as could be done. The fact is taken into consideration that the offense might have been committed because of a misunderstanding or through thoughtlessness and inexperience, or while under the pernicious influence of unpatriotic persons. They are therefore carefully instructed. . . . They are given ample time to reflect upon their actions and to come to an intelligent decision.

As a result, misunderstandings are usually cleared up. Objections are removed and . . . they voluntarily and cheerfully decide to enter the service. . . . Of the fifty men sent here as slackers within the past two months, not one has been tried and condemned. A practical solution in each case was found and, with the few exceptions of those who were found mentally incapacitated, all are now on duty with the colors. [23]

The COs confined at Alcatraz related far different stories. Philip Grosser stated that as soon as he arrived on the island, he was ordered by a sergeant to go to work. He promptly ignored the order and was sentenced to fourteen days in solitary confinement "and a bread and water diet."

> The overseer in charge switched on the electric light and took me down a flight of stairs to the basement, hollowed out of the rock under the prison. He ordered me to take up a bucket . . . he showed me into a cell, locked the iron barred door behind me, and I heard his footsteps going up the stairs as I was left alone in the dungeon. Then he switched off the lights and I found myself in complete darkness.
>
> The air in the cell was stagnant, the walls were wet and slimy, the bars of the cell door were rusty with dampness, and the darkness was so complete that I could not make out my hand a few inches before my face.[24]

Other prisoners reported similar treatment. When four Hutterite objectors arrived on Alcatraz in 1918, they refused to put on the military-issue uniforms offered by the guards. "Then they were taken to the dungeon into the dark, dirty, stinking cells for solitary confinement. The uniforms were thrown down next to them with the warning, If you don't give in, you'll stay here till [sic] you die . . ."[25]

By some accounts, prisoners were sometimes confined with their hands shackled above their heads to the bars of the cell doors.[26] Eventually, media exposure and public concern forced the army to put an end to this practice, and it was outlawed on December 6, 1919.[27] Treatment for the objectors was still rugged, though, especially when "Bolshevik literature" was found in their possession, smuggled in by radical activist visitors.

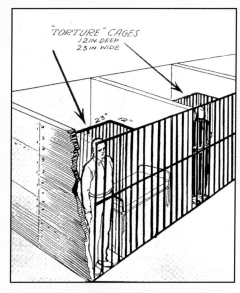

In January 1920, the Disciplinary Barracks installed so-called "torture cages" when the Secretary of War outlawed the army's earlier punishment of chaining convicts in a standing position to the bars of their cells. Euphemistically titled "vestibule doors," these cells were used for confining recalcitrant prisoners for 8-hour stretches. Public outcry led to the cells' abandonment within a few months.

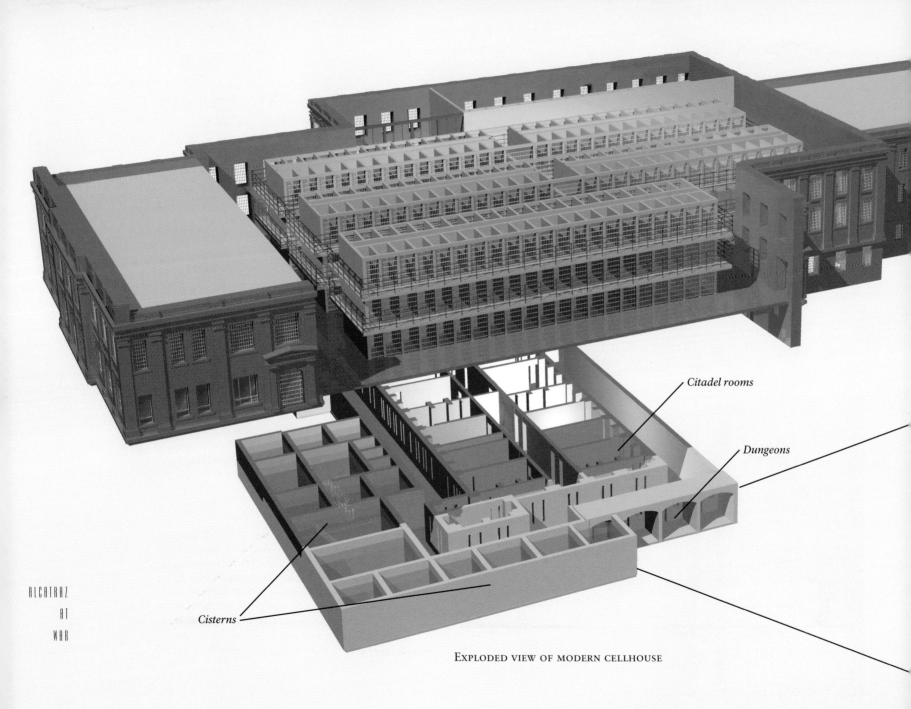

Citadel rooms

Dungeons

Cisterns

EXPLODED VIEW OF MODERN CELLHOUSE

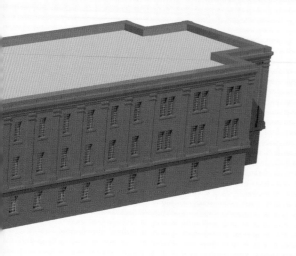

Perhaps the most notorious prisoner housed on the island during the Great War was neither a soldier nor a slacker, but rather the former German Consul General to San Francisco, Herr Franz Bopp. During 1916 and 1917, Bopp had become embroiled in a "German–Hindu Conspiracy," whose goal was the upsetting of British control of India. The marvelously Byzantine plot involved attempts by German and Hindu nationals in the US to ship arms to revolutionaries in India as well as mounting a propaganda campaign aimed at provoking mutiny among Indian soldiers in the British army. Germany, wishing to weaken its foe, also provided funds to members of the Indian independence movement.[28]

The plot was uncovered and Bopp and his vice consul, E. H. von Shack, were imprisoned on Alcatraz during their trials and convictions for violating pre-war neutrality laws. Bopp and von Shack spent six months in the Disciplinary Barracks before being transferred to the federal penitentiary at McNeill Island, Washington, to serve four-year sentences.[29]

By late 1920, the last of the slackers and the Hindu–German conspirators had been transferred from the Rock, and the Disciplinary Barracks resumed its role of housing only military convicts for the next thirteen years.

When the army constructed the present prison beginning in 1908, the upper stories of the old citadel were demolished to make way for the new building. However, the citadel's bottom floor and adjacent underground water cisterns were left behind to serve the needs of the new prison. Several of the former citadel rooms, located directly beneath the cellblocks, were earmarked for conversion to solitary confinement cells (see detail). These cells and the labyrinth of adjacent rooms provided the basis for innumerable tales of "Spanish tunnels" dug into the island's rock.

This photograph, taken in 1933, is the only known view showing the solitary confinement cells located in the basement of the old citadel.

The Dripping Dungeons

Stories of dungeons deep within Alcatraz have persisted since the Rock's earliest days as a military post. Supposedly located somewhere below the island's tide line, rumor had it that these cells were hell-holes of pitch black darkness, dripping ceilings, and rusty bars dating back to Spanish days. The reality of solitary confinement in the Disciplinary Barracks was slightly different, but yields some clues into this persistent Alcatraz myth.

The army always set aside special cells on Alcatraz for isolating troublesome prisoners, and originally these cells were in the basement of the citadel atop the island. As the Lower Prison expanded following the Civil War, one wing of the guardhouse was remodeled into dungeon rooms (i.e., solitary confinement cells) for recalcitrant inmates.

When the army constructed the present Alcatraz cellhouse between 1908 and 1912, they tore down the upper stories of the citadel and converted its basement level into the solitary confinement area for the new prison. There, eight rooms originally designed as storehouses back in the 1850s were converted to dungeons by replacing their old wooden doors with barred iron grates. These were the rooms that housed the conscientious objectors of World War I as well as untold numbers of military prisoners and, later, federal penitentiary convicts.

The dungeons were finally abandoned in 1940, but not before the stories surrounding them had reached mythical levels. Chained in the dark underbelly of the cellhouse, prisoners' minds ran wild. One of the most persistent stories had it that the cells constantly dripped water, a difficult fact to reconcile with the dungeon's location 140 feet above the bay. As it turns out, one of the cells backed against an underground cistern, and it is likely that water seeped through the brick walls into this cell and condensed on its walls and ceiling. The basement was already damp from the rusty plumbing overhead, and the moisture oozing in through the walls must have made the image of underwater confinement terrifyingly real, at least in the prisoners' imaginations.

With the San Francisco skyline as a backdrop, young GIs from the 216th Coast Artillery regiment man a 40mm antiaircraft gun mounted atop the guards' apartment house on the parade ground. The 216th was a National Guard unit from Minnesota called into "regular" service in 1940 as part of the army's pre-war mobilization.

6 World War II

Use extreme care in seeing that by no chance tools, guns, knives, ammunition, or other articles which could possibly be used in an escape or riot get into the possession of the inmates.

Warden's instructions to the Coast Artillery, June 1942 [30]

ALCATRAZ ISLAND ON DECEMBER 7, 1941, was a very different prison from the one experienced by thousands of soldiers over the preceding eighty years. The army had shut down the Disciplinary Barracks in 1933 and transferred control of the island to the Department of Justice the following year. Extensively remodeled by the Bureau of Prisons to house the country's most incorrigible federal convicts, the prison's latest incarnation was "United States Penitentiary, Alcatraz Island." It was already indelibly etched in the American mind as the infamous "Rock" of tawdry crime novels and Hollywood's B movies.

Warden James A. Johnston heard the news of the attack on Pearl Harbor late in the morning of December 7 and decided on how best to inform the convict population:

> Immediately after hearing the radio flash of what had happened at Pearl Harbor . . . I wrote it out, just as it was announced, hurried into the cellhouse, and had it chalked up on a bulletin blackboard which I put at the entrance to the dining hall. The prisoners had just come in from the yard where they had had the usual Sunday morning baseball games. As the prisoners lined up ready for the signal to enter the mess

Ripley's "Believe It Or Not" gave its own unique spin to Alcatraz's history in 1945.

Right
Soldiers training with antiaircraft machine guns "somewhere on the Pacific Coast" in the early months of World War II. The devastation at Pearl Harbor demonstrated the threat posed by Japanese planes, and the military hurriedly erected scores of antiaircraft defenses around West Coast cities, harbors, and industrial areas.

Opposite
Alcatraz Penitentiary's laundry and workshops were part of the government's "Federal Prison Industries" agency, and before the war the island's convicts did laundry for army posts and manufactured furniture, rubber mats, shoes, and prison garb for other federal institutions.

Clockwise from upper left
The interior of the laundry on the second floor of the Industries Building; the original dry cleaning plant at the northern end of the island. In 1940-1941 these two buildings were replaced by "New" Industries Building (see page 63); a convict applies red lead primer to one of the flotation buoys for the antisubmarine net that stretched across the Golden Gate during the war; and cargo nets for the navy being woven in the net shop in the ground floor of the Industries Building.

hall they read the news—read as all the rest of us read it—surprised, shocked, stunned, stirred.

And when the infamy of it all was grasped, and the tragedy of it all was understood, and the consequences of it all calculated, like all the rest of us they realized that we were cemented, united and ready for the work and the sacrifices that might be necessary.[31]

Nerves were on razor edge. San Francisco experienced its first air raid drill on December 8, when over-zealous observers mistakenly thought they spotted enemy aircraft coming in from the Pacific. Someone at the army's Western Defense Command hit the air raid sirens announcing a blackout, but the city's lights blazed on. The next day, the *San Francisco Chronicle* reported that "blacked-out San Francisco looked like New Orleans at Mardi Gras time."[32] General John DeWitt at the Presidio was furious and thundered his rage at the

Laundry

Dry Cleaning Plant

Net Shop

Painting flotation buoy

Before the start of the war, the Mat Shop was a major industrial area on Alcatraz where convicts cut old tires into strips and reworked them into rubber mats for navy shipboard use. In early 1942 Warden Johnston converted this area into the Net Shop.

mayor. He was convinced that Japanese planes had flown over San Francisco—yet the city had not blacked out!

"No bombs fell, did they?'" Mayor Angelo J. Rossi observed gently.

"It might have been better if bombs had dropped to awaken this city," DeWitt snapped. "I never saw such apathy. It was criminal. . . . It was shameful."[33]

Alcatraz Island was conspicuous by its brilliance that night, dozens of floodlights illuminating the prison walls. One guard remembered that the island "glowed like a Christmas tree."[34] General DeWitt considered it especially outrageous that the federal facility hadn't complied with blackout regulations; he reportedly ordered Alcatraz's lights shot out if the penitentiary didn't comply in the future. It required intervention at the level of the Department of Justice to get Warden Johnston to follow the general's directives.[35]

Johnston didn't allow the blackout controversy to get in the way of defense work, though, and he immediately put the island's industries on a war footing. The penitentiary had been operating a laundry and carpentry shop since its opening in 1934 to support military bases around the bay, and he correctly figured that the importance of the island's industries would increase exponentially as San Francisco geared up for war. Johnston quickly negotiated agreements with the War Department to provide a variety of new services.

In addition to expanding the laundry to handle increased military loads, the prison's Tailor Shop switched over from producing convict uniforms to manufacturing army jackets, pants, and caps. Sometimes the war industries required unique skills. The navy had a critical need for oversized cargo nets used in loading freight aboard ships, so a Net

The New Industries Building (right), constructed by the Bureau of Prisons on the former site of the island's rock quarry and dry cleaning plant. The block-long building contained various manufacturing shops on the first floor and the island's sprawling laundry on the second. In the distance outside the fence is the former army Model Shop Building, abandoned in 1941.

From 1942 to 1945 the Tailor Shop turned out military uniform items for the army and marine corps. During the war, prisoners earned from 5¢ to 12¢ per hour for working in the Prison Industries and reinvested heavily in War Bonds. Warden Johnston reported in 1943 that some cons were putting 90 percent of their tiny earnings into bonds.

Shop was set up, and convicts learned to weave jute strands into netting under the tutelage of a seasoned boson's mate. The shop turned out thousands of nets during the war and earned a navy commendation for its war production efforts.

Johnston also instituted new pay scales for the inmates. The men were divided into four categories based on skill and responsibilities, with salaries ranging from 5 cents to 12 cents per hour. Many of the men promptly invested their earnings in war bonds.[36]

Just before Pearl Harbor, the navy had begun stretching an anti-submarine net across the harbor. Anchored to the bottom by huge concrete blocks, the net was a 6,000-ton metal blanket that stretched three miles across the bay from Sausalito to the San Francisco Marina.[37] It was suspended on the surface by large cylindrical buoys that took a terrible beating in the bay's currents, and Johnston arranged to have them brought to the island for overhaul. The damaged buoys were pulled up by the navy and transported to the island by barge. They were then trucked to a flat area at the north end of the island for scraping, sandblasting, patching, and repainting.

Aside from its war-related industries, Alcatraz again became a critical defensive position. Early in 1942 the Western Defense Command ordered that a battery of antiaircraft guns be sent to the island. Details for the new installation were swiftly worked out between the army and the Department of Justice, and in late spring, construction began on four gun emplacements.

Details of the design and construction of the emplacements were left to Colonel Sclick of the 216th Coast Artillery Regiment. The battery would consist of four 40mm antiaircraft guns sited to provide

In 1941, the original army D Block in the cellhouse was demolished and replaced by a state-of-the-art cellblock. The new block, shown here under construction, replaced the legendary dungeons below the cellhouse floor in the remains of the citadel. The new D Block was officially known as Isolation, Segregation, or the Treatment Unit, but to convicts it was still "the Hole."

all-around fields of fire from the island. Two guns were located at either end of the cellhouse roof; another gun was emplaced on top of the three-story Model Shop at the north end of the island; and the last weapon sat atop the solarium penthouse of the guards' apartment building at the south end of the island. As a camouflage measure, carpenters constructed four-foot-high wooden walls around each gun and painted the enclosures to blend with the buildings. Construction crews arrived in early June and within two weeks the guns were emplaced and ready for their crews.[38]

Responsibility for the Alcatraz battery was assigned to Battery F of the 216th Coast Artillery Regiment, a National Guard unit from Minnesota commanded by Captain Harry Freeman.[39] His first visit to the island took place just as construction was being completed on the new emplacements. When he paid a formal call on the warden, much to his relief, Freeman found Johnston to be a thoroughly professional administrator, and not at all opposed to a military presence on his island. The warden had no problem with the antiaircraft battery, he told Freeman, as long as the weapons and their crews didn't interfere with prison operations.

Top
A correctional officer poses with the "Blood Donor Record" that kept tally of the prison staff's wartime blood donations. For a while, convicts and guards maintained an unofficial but intense donor rivalry. The guard staff was hampered in their donation frequency by physical fitness standards, but some officers still managed to surpass the respected Gallon Mark.

Bottom
Warden James Johnston (seated, lower left) and other Bureau of Prisons officials at a wartime Prison Industries conference.

Nearly fifty years later, the only truly unique thing Harry remembered about the visit with Johnston was the convict trusty, who stood silently in the dining room and served them lunch.[40]

Guarding San Francisco's shoreline from the Golden Gate Bridge to the Embarcadero had already stretched Battery F thin. Manning the battery on Alcatraz was an additional duty and for several days the defense of the island became a commuter operation. Each morning, Freeman trucked soldiers from the Presidio to Fort Mason, where they caught a boat to the island. Lunch came out on the noontime boat, and at night the men returned to their barracks in the Presidio. The army hadn't placed any searchlights on the island for night firing, so its

The New Industries Building on Alcatraz under construction in 1940. This building was one of a number of improvements to the island funded by the federal government's Public Works Administration (PWA) during 1940-1941. Other PWA construction on Alcatraz included new apartments for the guards and their families, an overhaul of the island's utility systems, and a state-of-the-art solitary confinement cellblock—D Block—in the main prison building.

A 40mm antiaircraft gun being hoisted to the roof of the prison hospital wing. This gun sat directly over the convict's recreation yard, so special nets were rigged to catch any objects falling from the gun emplacement.

defense became strictly a daylight affair. Freeman assigned Second Lieutenant Hiram H. Griffith to provide on-site liaison with the penitentiary staff. A dapper young officer who sported slicked-back hair and a pencil-thin mustache, Griffith was assigned quarters in the guards' apartment house. The lieutenant was eventually joined by a permanent detachment of soldiers from Battery D of the 216th Coast Artillery, who moved into the solarium penthouse atop the married guards' apartment building. This room was directly below one of the antiaircraft gun emplacements and the soldiers quickly converted it into a barracks, complete with GI beds and lockers.[41]

On June 18, Warden Johnston wrote a welcoming letter to the soldiers and issued them a mimeographed sheet titled "Regulations for Gun Crews." These rules included repeated references to maintaining security around the prisoners, including such obvious points as "Care will be taken that no tools, knives, equipment, or ammunition fall from gun positions." There were other special guidelines: magazines and newspapers were to be destroyed, and any contact or conversation with the prisoners was strictly prohibited. Johnston kept the convicts isolated from most news of the outside world, and the soldiers were not going to be an accidental conduit to that type of information.

The prisoners' only official source of war news came from the edited dispatches shared with them by the warden. The prison grapevine filled in the rest. The convicts were very aware of the presence of an armed military presence on the island and speculated about their mission. One theory held that the antiaircraft guns were merely dummy weapons meant to divert Japanese bombers from real military targets elsewhere on the bay. Inmate Jim Quillen recalled one especially vicious rumor:

This view from the lighthouse clearly shows the antiaircraft gun emplacement atop the administration wing of the prison building. Notice how the exterior of its wooden enclosure was painted to match the prison's masonry walls. The temporary tarpaper structures nearby held reserve ammunition and a "ready room" for the gun crew. Access to the gun emplacements on the prison was via a temporary wooden staircase built against the façade. The staircase had a locked door at its base, the key to which was kept by the soldiers on the roof and lowered on a string to relief crews coming up the stairs.

Top
Three of the island's teenage girls posed on the army truck named "Betsy Ann." From left to right, Anne Folksdorf, Betty Weinhold, and Joyce Rose. Years later, Joyce recalled that shortly after Warden Johnston issued formal guidelines to the soldiers, he held a meeting with the guards, telling them in less formal terms how he expected their daughters to behave around the troops.

Bottom
The Lover's Bench at the southern tip of the island was a favorite spot for island residents' snapshots. In this view, a soldier from the antiaircraft battery and a Coast Guardsman from the light-house, dressed in his wartime navy uniform, join Alcatraz children and teens on the bench.

If an invasion came, the guards would kill inmates in their cells rather than let the Japanese set them free.[42]

The order prohibiting contact between the soldiers and prisoners seems to have been widely ignored, at least according to inmate Alvin "Old Creepy" Karpis. In his memoirs, Karpis claimed that the soldiers' attitude toward the cons was downright friendly: "Whenever possible they throw cigarettes and sandwiches down into the yard and exchange casual stories." He also recorded an exchange between one of the guards and the Coast Artillery troops:

> "Punch-Drunk" Pepper marches along the wall, practicing manual-of-arms movements with his rifle. He attempts, between his private drill practice, to write up the soldiers for fraternizing with the prisoners. The servicemen respond bluntly, "Go f—k yourself! Get away from here!"[43]

The soldiers soon blended into the routine of family life on Alcatraz. They were granted full membership in the island's Officers' Club (correctional officers, that is), given canteen privileges in the tiny grocery store, and invited to dances and parties in the guards' homes. A few flirtations blossomed between the GIs and the resident daughters, and the soldiers named their truck "Betsy Ann" in honor of two Alcatraz girls.[44]

As time went on, defense of the island became first routine, and then downright boring. By 1944, it was obvious that Japanese planes were about as likely as pterodactyls to appear over San Francisco, and the Coast Artillery began shipping men overseas for frontline duty. On July 26, Warden Johnston informed the Director of the Bureau of Prisons, James Bennett, that all four guns and their associated equipment had been removed from their emplacements, and that the wooden enclosures and crew's ready rooms on the buildings would be demolished shortly.[45] Bennett instructed Johnston to see if he could scrounge any wood from the emplacements for use elsewhere on the island and opined about the military, "I was surprised that the army kept those now more-or-less obsolete antiaircraft guns on the Island as long as they have. I am glad to know that they have decided to take them down and perhaps utilize the personnel a little bit more realistically." In a surge of patriotism and good will, Bennett also demanded the army "repair" any damage which had been done to the institution roofs or the officers' quarters or "anything else which they used."[46]

It is not recorded how—or even if—the soldiers responded to Director Bennett's admonition to pick up after themselves following two years of protecting the island and its occupants from possible attack. Likely they had more pressing matters on their minds.

Shortly afterward, the navy removed its submarine net from the bay and with it, the need to have Alcatraz inmates overhaul the flotation buoys. For the remaining months of the war, Alcatraz's inmates focused mostly on uniform production, net weaving, and laundry washing. (Wartime soldiers, upon learning that their laundry was sent to Alcatraz, used to brag "Al Capone does my shorts," despite the fact that the crime czar had been gone from the island since 1940.)

After his retirement, Warden Johnston wrote of the prisoners' wartime contributions: "Man for man, they compared favorably with the rank and file of citizens in producing goods for the Army, Navy, Marine Corps, Maritime and Transportation Service. Regardless of what they have done or may do, I like to record and remember them at their best—when they were working to win the war."[47]

Alcatraz soldiers and teenagers display the catch of the day hauled from the island's dock: a leopard shark.

A Wartime Escape

Prisoners had been trying to escape from Alcatraz from nearly the first moment the army opened the place for business. The first recorded attempts began during the Civil War as soldier-prisoners tried to escape the embryonic prison and make their way to San Francisco. A local paper recorded a typical incident in June 1862 when a prisoner named John D. Wood "by some unknown means left the cells last night, and obtained a small boat about 12 o'clock, and with two others, left for purposes unknown." The island's commanding officer must have felt personally insulted; he offered a $30 reward from his own pocket for Wood's recapture.[48]

Such attempts continued throughout the military's 75-year tenure on the island, and the army documented at least eighty men trying to escape in twenty-nine separate attempts. Of these, sixty-two were caught, one may have drowned, and seventeen were "unknown."

Interestingly, these incidents didn't usually involve swimming the bay's frigid waters. Most escapees simply fled mainland work crews and never even got their feet wet. Those army prisoners who did try to escape from the island proper generally attempted to float to the mainland on buoyant objects ranging in seaworthiness from small boats to bundles of driftwood. Sometimes the army's prisoners used more creative routes such as forging their own release papers or, in one memorable case, hiding in a packing crate and having themselves shipped off the island as freight. (This last attempt resulted in only a few hours of off-island freedom.)

Perhaps one of the most creative attempts occurred during World War II, when a 50-year-old train robber named John K. Giles managed to get off the island and actually made it to the mainland. (Well, to another island, anyway.) Giles had been sent to Alcatraz after escaping from Oregon State Prison and attempting to knock over a mail shipment—a federal offense. Once on the island, the skinny, aging convict didn't appear to be much of an escape risk so the staff gave him a job working on the prison dock. Not strong enough for the heavy labor of manhandling cargo and bundles of military laundry, Giles was put to work sweeping the dock and tending the flower gardens near the steps to the guards' apartments.

The vast quantities of military laundry crossing the dock soon caught Giles' attention, and over the course of several weeks he managed to pilfer enough army clothing to put together a complete sergeant's uniform. At this time late in the war, the penitentiary was upgrading its phone system with the assistance of the US Army Signal Corps, and there was a constant stream of military technicians arriving and departing the island.

On July 31, 1945, Giles went to work on the island dock where he ducked out of view, donned his stolen army uniform, put on his convict coveralls over the uniform, and resumed his regular cleanup chores. At about 10 o'clock the little army transport *General Frank M. Coxe* pulled up at the island on her morning run. Giles jumped under the dock, stripped off his coveralls, and stepped into an open cargo door on the *Coxe*'s lower deck. The transport then departed on the next leg of her regular schedule.

As soon as the *Coxe* cast off her moorings, the correctional officer supervising the dock crew took a head count and came up one convict short. He glanced at the departing transport and felt a knot in his stomach as if he'd eaten a very bad meatball. Phone calls began to fly between the dock and the prison building, where the associate warden was observed running through the admin offices yelling as he went "Giles is missing from the dock—he may be on the *Coxe*!" The captain of the guard loaded up a speedboat with a crew of officers and sped ahead to the *Coxe*'s next stop at Fort McDowell on Angel Island.[49]

Sources disagree about what happened next. History is frequently like that. According to the warden, he called ahead to Angel Island and requested that the army detain any unaccounted-for passengers until his guards arrived. According to one of the Alcatraz guards, though, the speedboat arrived ahead of the *Coxe* and the correctional officers scrutinized the soldiers as they departed at Fort McDowell. Giles, stepping off the transport and faced with a lineup of

JOHN K. GILES
NO. 250—AZ
U. S. P.
ALCATRAZ ISLAND

"Sergeant" John Giles, back on Alcatraz after his AWOL trip to Angel Island.

BOAT FELON HID ON

Corporal Paul Lorinz (left) and Sergeant Shirley Casey point to lower deck of Army ferryboat General Coxe on which John K. Giles hid after escape from Alcatraz today. On upper deck is Deck Hand Jerry Van Soest; below, Oiler Jim Saunders. Lorinz spotted Giles as prisoner despite the fact he was wearing Army uniform and Giles was seized when ferry put in at Angel Island. —Call-Bulletin Photograph.

all-too-familiar guard faces, reportedly muttered, "I thought that god-damned tub was headed for San Francisco."[50]

Giles was taken back to Alcatraz, where a full-length photo was taken of him in army uniform, probably for use as evidence at his inevitable trial for attempted escape. Except for his rumpled appearance and hangdog countenance, Giles in his technical sergeant's uniform looked very much the part of a senior enlisted soldier, perhaps one of the "thirty-year men" still serving in the army during the last days of World War II. Had the *Coxe* been headed to San Francisco instead of Angel Island, he might well have disappeared into the hordes of military men then in the city.

Officially, John Giles had five more years added to his Alcatraz sentence for this little stunt. Unofficially, many on the guard staff actually admired the wiry con's gall and felt that instead of increasing his sentence, he should have gotten a reward of some sort.

But that was off the record, off course.

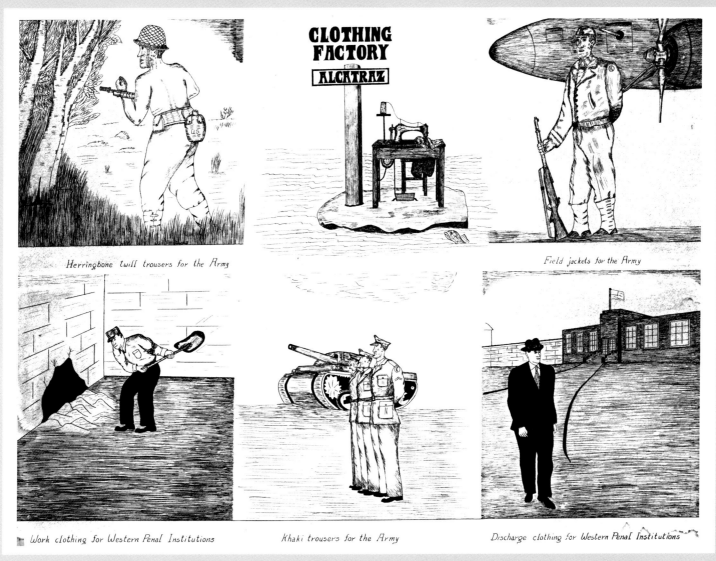

The artwork may not have been of the highest caliber, but the patriotism is obvious in this series of drawings done by Alcatraz inmate James Widmer to illustrate wartime clothing production.

Epilogue

MOST OF THE PHYSICAL REMINDERS of Alcatraz at war disappeared from the island decades ago. Smoothbore cannon no longer poke their snouts over brick parapets; the cobbled-together penal slums known as Upper and Lower prisons have long since been demolished; and the dungeon rooms below the main cellhouse were ripped out in 1940. Even the Coast Artillery's antiaircraft gun emplacements of World War II have disappeared without trace. Little remains visible today to hint at the wartime history of Alcatraz and the soldiers and prisoners who spent much of their lives there. Except, perhaps, for their graffiti.

Soldiers love to leave their marks where they've been posted, and Alcatraz was no exception. If one looks long enough in the underground chambers dotting the island, one

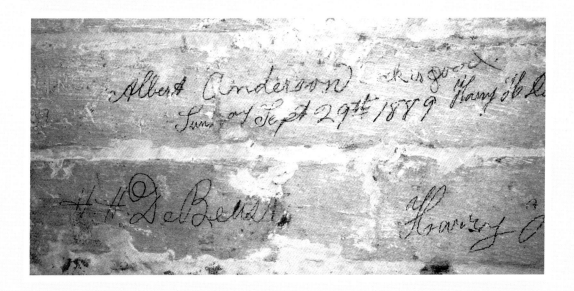

will find the penciled sketches and scratched notes of soldiers who once lived—or were confined—within its walls. Usually these messages are simple recordings of names, dates, units, or hometowns: "Albert Herrin July 1887," "Scranton Penn," "Harry Thomas 3rd Co D.B.G. 1920." Sometimes the message is triumphant: "5107 Discharged—June 15 1912." On occasion, though, the messages are nothing more than wistful illustrations of a life gone-by, such as a patriotic eagle bearing an *e pluribus unum* pennant; a soldier wearing an 1890s campaign hat; a long-horned steer; and women in various stages of period dress— and undress.

Most common, though, are the convicts' registry numbers. These numbers, assigned to each arriving prisoner, were often used by the cons themselves as a self-deprecatory way of identification. Though covered with layer upon layer of whitewash, the numbers can usually be found carved deep into the brick walls of the former dungeon rooms. Frequently, an abbreviated date follows these numbers, possibly representing the convicts' sentences or time left to serve: "11557 5yrs 2mos," "11645 3yrs 7mos." No one will ever know the meaning for sure since no military convicts confined in the dungeons are known to still be alive.

For researchers, these scrawls are tantalizing and frustrating fragments of history. Although voluminous records exist for the infamous Alcatraz Penitentiary and its convict population, no official files have survived for prisoners serving time in the army's Disciplinary Barracks. Their official records were destroyed long ago during military housecleaning efforts. Only their graffiti marks these men's stay on the Rock.

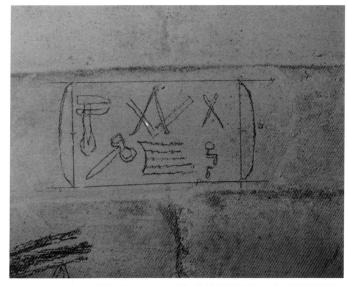

A lonely-looking Rodman gun peers out from the Alcatraz parade ground during the 1920s, while a pair of ferryboats shuttle past a pre-bridge Golden Gate.

The End of the Guns

The high-water mark for artillery on Alcatraz was reached shortly after the Civil War, by which time more than a hundred cannon were emplaced in the island's batteries. However, the vast majority of these guns—aging smoothbore weapons dating back to the 1840s—had been rendered effectively useless by advances in military technology. In the late 1860s, US Army Engineers began stripping Alcatraz of most of its armament and undertaking a complete remodeling of the island's fortifications.

By 1876 only a handful guns remained mounted on Alcatraz, all of them 15-inch Rodmans still considered to be effective against ironclad warships. Throughout the rest of the nineteenth century, the number of emplaced (i.e., defensive) cannon dwindled even further until the Spanish–American War, when the island's active armament consisted only of a pair of rifled 8-inch guns positioned for defense of the bay's minefields; the guns had not been mounted when the war was in its active phase.

When the War Department finally redesignated Alcatraz as a US Military Prison in 1907, the few cannon remaining on the island were reduced to the ignoble roles of roadway barricades or parade ground decorations.

Right
An article in the March 1920 issue of Popular Mechanics *illustrated how the army scrapped many of the guns still on the island. According to the accompanying story, the demolition of the so-called "old Naval guns" also blew out the windows in the powerhouse.*

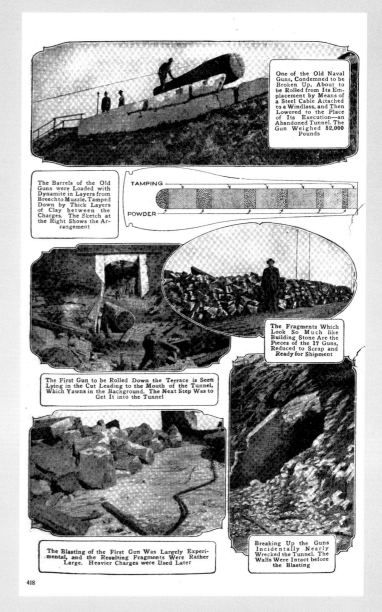

One of the Old Naval Guns, Condemned to be Broken Up, About to be Rolled from Its Emplacement by Means of a Steel Cable Attached to a Windlass, and Then Lowered to the Place of Its Execution—an Abandoned Tunnel. The Gun Weighed 52,000 Pounds

The Barrels of the Old Guns were Loaded with Dynamite in Layers from Breech to Muzzle, Tamped Down by Thick Layers of Clay between the Charges. The Sketch at the Right Shows the Arrangement

TAMPING
POWDER

The Fragments Which Look So Much like Building Stone Are the Pieces of the 17 Guns, Reduced to Scrap and Ready for Shipment

The First Gun to be Rolled Down the Terrace is Seen Lying in the Cut Leading to the Mouth of the Tunnel, Which Yawns in the Background. The Next Step Was to Get It into the Tunnel

The Blasting of the First Gun Was Largely Experimental, and the Resulting Fragments Were Rather Large. Heavier Charges were Used Later

Breaking Up the Guns Incidentally Nearly Wrecked the Tunnel. The Walls Were Intact before the Blasting

418

In 1920 the army hit upon a unique solution for scrapping these unwieldy gun barrels, many of which weighed upwards of 50,000 pounds: Workers hauled the weapons into an unused island tunnel, packed them with dynamite, and blew the guns into manageable chunks of scrap iron.

When the Bureau of Prisons assumed control of Alcatraz in 1933, only three guns remained on the island: a miniscule salute gun facing the Golden Gate and a pair of 8-inch rifled Rodman guns set into the ornamental rock wall surrounding the parade ground. (The latter were apparently the same two intended for minefield defense during the Spanish–American War.) Over the next decade, the aging cannon became a common backdrop for island snapshots, especially the Rodman next to the so-called Lover's Bench at the southern tip of the island.

During World War II, the residents of Alcatraz eagerly participated in wartime scrap drives, scavenging the island for every bit of usable metal. During one of these campaigns, it was suggested that the three army guns on the parade ground would go a long way toward defeating the Axis, and the cannon were dragged to the island's dock, where they joined a mountain of old radiators, cell doors, water pipes, and boiler fittings also waiting to do their bit for the war effort. Hauled away by scrap barge in 1942, no one knows the final fate of the island's guns: did they become key components of tanks destined for the Normandy beaches? Or, as was frequently the case with salvaged cannon, did the Alcatraz guns simply gather rust until after the war, only to become the Frigid-Aires, Buick Roadmasters, and manhole covers of post-World War II America?

Alcatraz's last three cannon await their fates on the island dock, 1942.

Sources Cited

1. National Archives [NA], Cartographic Archives Division, RG 77, Office of the Chief of Engineers [OCE], Fortifications File, Drawer 95-107, "Field Map of 'Isla de los Alcatrazes' San Francisco Harbor . . ." May 1847.

2. Watkinds, T.H. and R. R. Olmsted. *Mirror of the Dream: An Illustrated History of San Francisco*. San Francisco: Scrimshaw Press, 1976.

3. Galvin, John, editor. *The Journal of Juan Manuel de Ayala. The First Ship Into San Francisco Bay, 1775*. San Francisco: John Howell Books, 1971.

4. Martini, John A. *Fortress Alcatraz: Guardian of the Golden Gate*. Kailua, Hawaii: Pacific Monographs, 1991.

5. NA, RG 77, OCE, "Report relative to an examination of the Coast of the US on the Pacific by a Joint Commission of Navy and Army Officers," Nov. 1, 1850, to Secretaries of War and Navy.

6. O.R., Series I, Volume L/1 (S#106) Union . . . Operations on the Pacific Coast From July 1, 1862 to June 30, 1865, R.C. Drumm, Adj. Gen, Dept of Pacific to Lt. Col Harvey Lee, CO, Benicia Barracks.

7. Manuscript, "The Alcatraz Letters of Charles Herzog, 3rd US Artillery, 1860-1861" in the Hauptstaatarchiv of Baden-Wuerttemberg, translated by Jutta von Weise.

8. NA, RG 94, AGO: NA, RG 393, Dept. of the Pacific, Letters Sent 1848-1866, Vol. 10, AAG R. Drumm, Aug. 26, 1861, to CO, Alcatraz.

9. Harpending, Asbury. *The Great Diamond Hoax and Other Stirring Episodes in the Life of Asbury Harpending: An Epic of Early California*. San Francisco: James H. Barry Co., 1913.

10. Herzog. In 1978, a portion of an exploded 8-inch Columbiad cannon was recovered from the Alcatraz tidepools. It is believed to be the weapon that almost killed Herzog.

11. O.R. Series 1, Volume L/1 (S#106) Union . . . Operations on the Pacific Coast From July 1, 1862 to June 30, 1865, Letter, Capt. William Winder to Lt. Col. R.D. Drumm, Asst. Adj. Gen., Dept. of the Pacific.

12. O.R. Series 1, Volume L/1 (S#106) Union . . . Operations on the Pacific Coast From July 1, 1862 to June 30, 1865, Letter, R. D. Drumm to Winder, CO, Alcatraz Island.

13. "Post Return for Alcatraz Island" October 1870

14. National Archives, RG 92, Office of the Quarter Master General, Consolidated Correspondence File, Alcatraz, Lt. G. L. Anderson, QM, Alcatraz, March 31, 1881, to Chief QM, Division of the Pacific.

15. Thompson, Erwin. "The Rock: A History of Alcatraz Island 1847-1972." Denver, CO: National Park Service, 1979.

16. NA, RG 92, OWMG, General Correspondence 1890-1914, Sect. of Interior Hoke Smith, Dec. 13, 1894, to Sect. of War; AG, Dec. 14, 1894 to CG, Dept. of Colorado, and Dec. 26, to CG, Dept. of Calif., CO, Alcatraz, Jan. 8, 1895, at AAG, Dept. of Calif.; and AG, Aug. 7, 1895, to CG, Dept. of Calif.

17. "Moquis on Alcatraz. They Rebelled Against Education." *San Francisco Call*, February 24, 1895.

18. Rickey, Don Jr. *Forty Miles a Day on Beans and Hay: The Enlisted Soldier Fighting the Indian Wars*. Norman: University of Oklahoma Press, 1963.

19. NA, RG 77, OCE, General Correspondence 189-1914, Maj. Gen. A. MacArthur, Nov. 9, 1903, to AG.

20. Thompson, "The Rock," p. 232.

21. Most historians today prefer the designation "Philippine–American War."

22. Grosser, Philip. *Uncle Sam's Devil's Island*. Place and publisher unknown, 1933.

23. "The Slacker Problem," *The Rock*, v. 3, no. 6, December 1917.

24. Grosser, pp. 11–12.

25. Ewert, J. George. "Christ or Country?" *The Plough*, no 4, May 1984, pp. 8–9.

26. Ewert, p. 8.

27. Grosser, p. 21.

28. NA, RG 118, NEUVIO, US vs Franz Bopp, Ram Chandra, et al, 1913–1920.

29. *San Francisco Examiner*, November 17, 1917, and May 5, 1918.

30. NA, San Bruno, RG-129: Administrative Files: G-M—Air Raids and Blackouts.

31. Johnston, James A. *Alcatraz Island Prison and the Men Who Live There*. New York: Charles Scribner's Sons. 1949.

32. *San Francisco Chronicle*, December 9, 1941.

33. Nolte, Carl. "Infamy, War—and a Sea Change." *San Francisco Chronicle*, May 9, 1999.

34. Bergen, Philip. Interview, San Francisco, August 1987.

35. Bergen.

36. Johnston.

37. Laurence, Lorrie. "Tiburon's Submarine Net." *Marin Independent-Journal*, June 9, 1999.

38. NA, San Bruno, RG-129: Administrative Files: G-M—Air Raids and Blackouts, Correspondence, Warden Johnston to James V. Bennett, Director, Federal Bureau of Prisons, May 4, 1942; June 1, 1942; June 4, 1942; June 5, 1942; June 18, 1942.

39. The Artillery uses the word "battery" to refer to both a gun emplacement as well as to the men who manned the weapons. In the Infantry, this same group of soldiers is called a "company."

40. Freeman, Harry. Interviews, Corte Madera, California, May 1990; Mill Valley, California, June 2000.

41. NARA, San Bruno, RG-129, correspondence, Johnston to J. E. Overlade, Chief Accountant, Bureau of Prisons, June 25, 1942.

42. Quillen, James. Interview, Alcatraz Island, June 1990.

43. Karpis, Alvin and Robert Livesesy. *The Rock: Twenty-five Years On Alcatraz*. New York: Beaufort Books, 1980.

44. Ritz, Joyce. Interview, Alcatraz Island, February 1991.

45. NARA, San Bruno, RG-129, correspondence, Johnston to Bennett, July 26, 1944.

46. NARA, San Bruno, RG-129, correspondence, Bennett to Johnston, August 2, 1944.

47. Johnston.

48. *San Francisco Daily Evening Bulletin*, "A Desperate Soldier Escaped From Fort Alcatraz," 26 June 1862, p 3.

49. Johnston, *Alcatraz Island Prison*, pp. 205–206.

50. Bergen, Philip. Interviewed for the Discovery Channel documentary "Alcatraz." A La Carte Productions, 1999.

Acknowledgments

This book first took life at the suggestion of two good friends, Nicki Phelps and Susan Tasaki of the Golden Gate National Parks Association. When I began my retirement from the National Park Service in 1999, Nicki and Susan urged me to use my knowledge of Alcatraz's military history and write about life on the island during wartime. Although I had touched upon this theme briefly in my book *Fortress Alcatraz*, they both felt that the human aspects of wartime Alcatraz still needed to be properly told—stories overlooked by other authors whose works had focused primarily on the federal penitentiary—and thought that a book about Alcatraz at war could be richly illustrated with seldom-seen photographs from the National Park Service's archival collections. Both as a writer and a photographer, I was sold on their idea.

At the outset I wish to express my deepest thanks to Nicki and Susan for inspiring me to write *Alcatraz At War* and for their continued support as I searched through endless governmental and private collections around the country. A number of other people also provided me with inspiration and assistance during this process, especially my close friends Stephen Haller, the historian for the Golden Gate National Recreation Area, and Jolene Babyak, a former Alcatraz resident, author, and researcher extraordinaire. I also received tremendous assistance from various Alcatraz "alumni" who shared their stories with me of life on the island: Philip R. Bergen, former Captain of the Guard; Joyce Rose Ritz, who as a teenager witnessed the island's World War II activities; and Colonel Harry Freeman, who commanded Alcatraz's antiaircraft batteries in 1942.

I am also indebted to the staff at the San Francisco Public Library for their help, in particular to photographic archivist Pat Akre; to Susan Ewing-Haley and Kim Sulik at the National Park Service's Park Archives and Records Center at the Presidio; to the librarians and archivists at the J. Porter Shaw Library at Fort Mason; and to the staff at the Federal Archives and Records Center in San Bruno, especially Lisa Miller, who helped me sift through their exhaustive collection of Alcatraz records.

Finally, I wish to extend my respect and admiration to four people who helped me immensely but whom I can no longer thank in person, for they passed away during the writing of this book: Erica Toland, documents archivist at San Francisco Maritime National Historic Park; Walt Stack, former army prisoner and legendary San Franciscan; Jim Quillen, former penitentiary prisoner and great friend; and historian Erwin "T" Thompson, my mentor. The longer they are gone, the more questions I wish I could have asked.

To all, thank you very much.

John Martini
Fairfax, California

Photograph/Historical Illustration Sources

Photographs and historical illustrations are listed by page number in the order in which they appear. Each citation includes the source of the photographic print/historical illustration, followed by the accession number/collection name (when known) and the name of the originating institution (in cases where the image source and original archive are different).

Institutional Abbreviations
BL—Bancroft Library, University of California, Berkeley
MLA—Mennonite Library and Archives, Bethel College, North Newton, KS
NA—National Archives, Washington, D.C.
PARC—Park Archives and Records Center, National Park Service/Golden Gate National Recreation Area, San Francisco, CA
SFMNHP—San Francisco Maritime National Historical Park, San Francisco, CA
SFPL—San Francisco Public Library, San Francisco History Center, San Francisco, CA

p. ii: Collection of Michael Esslinger

p. v: PARC, Interpretive Negative Collection, GOGA 2316, neg. 86-C-6 (Lake County Museum, Waconda, IL)

p. vi: PARC, Interpretive Negative Collection, GOGA 2316, neg. 86-C-7 (Lake County Museum, Waconda, IL)

p. viii: SFMNHP, P83.170.108, Betty Wallar Collection

p. 1: Collection of Harry Freeman

p. 2: PARC, Interpretive Negative Collection, GOGA-2316, neg. 80-C-92

p. 3: SFMNHP, P83.170.263, Betty Wallar Collection

p. 4: PARC, Fort Point National Historic Site

p. 7: PARC, 89-E-7 (NA, RG 77)

p. 8 (all): PARC, Alcatraz Photos/1864, GOGA-3087, SC Range Box (NA, #77-5-12-178-5, -6)

p. 9: "The War of the Rebellion: A Compilation of Official Records of the Union and Confederate Armies," Washington, D. C.: US Government Printing Office, 1880.

p. 12: PARC

p. 13: BL, BANC PIC 1971.055.208

p. 14: BL, BANC PIC 1971.055.636

p. 17: PARC, Interpretive Media Box 3

p. 23: BL, BANC PIC 1971.055.320

p. 25: BL, BANC PIC 1905.17500 vol. 1:35

p. 26 (top left): SFPL

p. 28: PARC

p. 29: NA, RG 92, OQMG, General Correspondence, 1890–1914, photo 2 of 19

p. 30 (top, engraving): Collection of the author; (bottom): PARC

p. 31: PARC, Interpretive Negative Collection, GOGA 2316, neg. 76-92 (NA, RG 92)

p. 32: BL, BANC PIC 1971.055.679

p. 33: PARC, P80.182, album p. 9 (SFMNHP)

p. 34 (left): Collection of the author; (right) MLA, H. R. Voth Collection

p. 35: MLA, H. R. Voth Collection

p. 36: PARC, Interpretive Negative Collection, GOGA 2316, neg. 77-C-242 (NA, RG 92)

p. 39: PARC, Interpretive Negative Collection, GOGA 2316, neg. 77-C-248 (NA, RG 92)

p. 40: PARC, Interpretive Negative Collection, GOGA 2316, neg. 77-C-251

p. 42: PARC, 77-239 (NA, RG 92)

p. 43 (top left): PARC 84-C-37; (top right): PARC P80-182, album p. 11 (SFMNHP); (bottom right): SFMNHP, P89-052

p. 44 (all): PARC, Interpretive Negative Collection, GOGA, 2316; (middle/kitchen) neg. 77-C-247, (bottom/mess hall) neg. 76-C-122, (NA, RG 92)

p. 45: PARC, Interpretive Negative Collection, GOGA, 2316, neg. 77-C-145 (NA, RG 92, no. 223810)

p. 46: PARC, Interpretive Negative Collection, GOGA, 2316, neg. 76-C-121

p. 47: PARC, P80-182, album p. 4 (SFMNHP)

p. 48: SFPL, San Francisco Historical Photograph Collection, neg. 1283 (original no. AAC-9238)

p. 50 (top): PARC, Interpretive Negative Collection, GOGA 2316 (NA, RG 92); (bottom): Collection of Rod Crossley

p. 51 (top, visitor's pass): Collection of the author; (center): PARC, Interpretive Negative Collection, GOGA 2316, neg. 76-E-96

p. 53: *San Francisco Examiner*, 1920

p. 56: PARC, Interpretive Photos, Box 1 (SFPL)

p. 58: PARC, Interpretive Negative Collection, GOGA 2316, neg. 80-C-77

p. 59: Collection of the author

p. 60: PARC/PAM Prints Collection

p. 61 (all): SFMNHP, P83.170, Betty Wallar Collection (top left, .199; top right, .19; bottom left, .262; bottom right, .269)

p. 62: SFMNHP, P83.170.261, Betty Wallar Collection

p. 63: SFMNHP, P83.170.74, Betty Wallar Collection

p. 64: SFMNHP, P83.170.244, Betty Wallar Collection

p. 65: SFMNHP, P83.170.190, Betty Wallar Collection

p. 66 (top): SFMNHP, P80.150.13; (bottom): P83.170.301, Betty Wallar Collection

p. 67: NA, RG 129

p. 68: PARC, Interpretive Negative Collection, GOGA 2316, neg. 77-C-420

p. 69: SFMNHP, P83.170.71, Betty Wallar Collection

pp. 70–71: Collection of Joyce Ritz

pp. 72–74: NA, RG 129

p. 75: PARC, Mary M. Bowman Collection, (SFMNHP, P83.161.5n)

pp. 76–79: Collection of/taken by the author

p. 80: SFMNHP, P83.170.113, Betty Wallar Collection

p. 81: Collection of the author

p. 83: SFMNHP, P83.170.16, Betty Wallar Collection

John A. Martini, a recognized authority on the subject of Alcatraz Island during its military years and on American coastal defenses and fortifications, is a native Californian with a life-long interest in the history of the American West. A fourth-generation San Franciscan, John graduated from Saint Ignatius High School and then attended the University of Southern California, U.C. Berkeley, and San Francisco State University. He worked as a National Park Ranger for more than twenty-five years at such diverse locations as Fort Point National Historic Site, Alcatraz Island, the National Maritime Museum, the USS *Arizona* Memorial, the Presidio of San Francisco, and Teddy Roosevelt's estate at Sagamore Hill National Historic Site. John and his wife Betsy, a recreational therapist, live in Fairfax, California, where they share a house in the redwoods with two cats and a pair of pygmy goats.

Also by John Martini

PUBLICATIONS

Contributor to *American Seacoast Defenses: A Reference Guide*. Houston, Texas: Coastal Defense Study Group Press, 1999.

Fort Point: Sentry at the Golden Gate. San Francisco: Golden Gate National Parks Association, 1992.

Guide to the Presido of San Francisco. San Francisco: Golden Gate National Parks Association, 1992, revised 2001.

Fortress Alcatraz. Kailua, Hawaii: Pacific Monographs, 1991.

ARTICLES

"J.D. Givens: A Personal and Professional Biography." *Prologue: Quarterly of the National Archives and Records Administration* (Summer 2002).

"Survivor of the Plan of 1870: Battery Cavallo, Fort Baker." *Coastal Defense Study Group Journal* (February 2000).

"Battery Cavallo: From Cannons to Butterflies." *ParkNews Magazine*. (Spring 1999)

"Search and Destroy: The 1864 Alcatraz Photographs." *The Civil War Chronicles* (Winter Issue 1994) and *American Heritage Magazine* (November 1992).

"Surveying the Battleship *Arizona*." *After the Battle Magazine* (No. 45, Fall 1984).

"Diving Into History." *Pearl Harbor-Gram* (Fall 1982).